BTEC First
Health & Social Care

Alison Hetherington, Liz Rasheed, Linda Wyatt

HODDER
EDUCATION

This material has been endorsed by Edexcel and offers high quality support for the delivery of Edexcel qualifications.

Edexcel endorsement does not mean that this material is essential to achieve any Edexcel qualification, nor does it mean that this is the only suitable material available to support any Edexcel qualification. No endorsed material will be used verbatim in setting any Edexcel examination and any resource lists produced by Edexcel shall include this and other appropriate texts. While this material has been through an Edexcel quality assurance process, all responsibility for the content remains with the publisher.

Copies of official specifications for all Edexcel qualifications may be found on the Edexcel website – www.edexcel.org.uk

Orders: please contact Bookpoint Ltd, 130 Milton Park, Abingdon, Oxon OX14 4SB.
Telephone: (44) 01235 827720. Fax: (44) 01235 400454.
Lines are open from 9.00–5.00, Monday to Saturday, with a 24-hour message answering service.
You can also order through our website www.hoddereducation.co.uk.

British Library Cataloguing in Publication Data
A catalogue record for this title is available from the British Library.

ISBN: 978 0 340 97157 4

First Published 2008
Impression number   10 9 8 7 6 5 4 3 2 1
Year   2012 2011 2010 2009 2008

Artwork by Barking Dog Art
Cover photo © Moodboard/Superstock
Typeset by Servis Filmsetting Ltd, Manchester

Printed in Italy for Hodder Education, part of Hachette Livre UK, 338 Euston Road, London NW1 3BH.

What does 'the expert choice' mean for you?

We work with more examiners and experts than any other publisher

- Because we work with more experts and examiners than any other publisher, the very latest curriculum requirements are built into this course and there is a perfect match between your course and the resources that you need to succeed. We make it easier for you to gain the skills and knowledge that you need for the best results.

- We have chosen the best team of experts – including the people that mark the exams – to give you the very best chance of success; look out for their advice throughout this book: this is content that you can trust.

More direct contact with teachers and students than any other publisher

- We talk with more than 100,000 students every year through our student conferences, run by Philip Allan Updates. We hear at first hand what you need to make a success of your A-level studies and build what we learn into every new course. Learn more about our conferences at **www.philipallan.co.uk**

- Our new materials are trialled in classrooms as we develop them, and the feedback built into every new book or resource that we publish. You can be part of that. If you have comments that you would like to make about this book, please email us at: **feedback@hodder.co.uk**

More collaboration with Subject Associations than any other publisher

- Subject Associations sit at the heart of education. We work closely with more Associations than any other publisher. This means that our resources support the most creative teaching and learning, using the skills of the best teachers in their field to create resources for you.

More opportunities for your teachers to stay ahead than with any other publisher

- Through our Philip Allan Updates Conferences, we offer teachers access to Continuing Professional Development. Our focused and practical conferences ensure that your teachers have access to the best presenters, teaching materials and training resources. Our presenters include experienced teachers, Chief and Principal Examiners, leading educationalists, authors and consultants. This course is built on all of this expertise.

Acknowledgements

I would like to thank my husband and children for their patience and support while I contributed to this book. I would also like to thank the staff I work with for their professional approach to maintaining the standards in health and social care education.

Liz Rasheed

I would like to thank my husband John for his support and my daughters Laura and Sally for their technical help and advice. Also my good friend Alison for her encouragement and advice. I would also like to thank my work colleagues at Mid Cheshire College for their support during the time I have spent researching and contributing to this exciting new book.

Alison Hetherington

I would like to thank my friends who have listened to me, made me many cups of tea and cooked dinner during the writing of this book, especially Kate, Nik, Harriet, Clair, Andy CP, Andy V, Jez and the DH'ers, especially Jo, Carmel and Ruth. Thanks are also due to my colleagues Kim and Maggie for their support. Lastly, I would like to acknowledge and thank Mike, Angela, Will and my parents for their continual love, support and encouragement.

Linda Wyatt

Introduction

We are teachers as well as vocational specialists and we value the BTEC approach, which combines theory with practice. If you are new to BTEC, either as a student or as a teacher, we hope you find this book helpful, interesting and a useful introduction to this vocational area. It is a distillation of our experience of teaching in health and social care but no one has all the answers. We would appreciate feedback and suggestions for improvement which we may incorporate into later editions.

Note to students – this is a textbook. Dip into it. Discuss it. Don't try to read it from cover to cover like a novel and please don't copy chunks out of it!

Liz Rasheed, Alison Hetherington and Linda Wyatt

> Remember, you should always respect the dignity and privacy of others when discussing placements, service users, or other health & social care experiences. When describing actual events, people, or settings, always keep names and identities anonymous.

Communication and Individual Rights within the Health and Social Care Sectors

People who work in health and social care need to be able to communicate well. This means they have to be good listeners as well as good at speaking in a way that others can understand. They have to listen to:

- patients in hospitals
- people who use social services (service users)
- relatives
- other professionals such as doctors, social workers, occupational therapists and many others who help to care for people.

Learning Outcomes

On completion of this unit you should be able to:

1 Investigate ways of promoting effective communication
2 Examine barriers to effective communication
3 Explore diversity and equality in society
4 Investigate how the principles of the care value base can be used to promote the rights of individuals and significant others.

The first part of the unit looks at communication skills, at difficulties that may occur with communication and how to overcome them. The second part of the unit looks at the role of the care worker in promoting rights. This means making sure people are given what they are entitled to. The care worker must ensure that people are given equal chances. Care workers need to understand that it is important to respect and value differences (diversity) when communicating with others.

This unit is mandatory, which means it is compulsory, for the First certificate and for the First diploma. Studying it at the start of the programme will help you communicate better when you are in work placement. This unit links with *Unit 4: Cultural Diversity in Health and Social Care.* It may help towards key skills communication.

1 Investigate ways of promoting effective communication

Forms of communication

So what is communication? Communication is a skill that we learn very early in life. Next time you see a baby, watch how it communicates. Assuming the baby is only a few weeks old, it will not able to speak. Babies learn to communicate very early, by crying when they need something.

What do you think these babies are communicating?

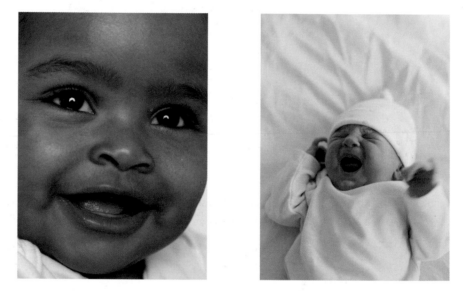

Are they tired? Unhappy? Happy? How do you know? Did you look at their faces? Babies and young children are effective (good) at communicating because their lives depend on it. They communicate when they are hungry or tired or uncomfortable. They also communicate when they are happy.

We use different ways to send messages. Babies use pre-language, making babbling and cooing sounds when happy and crying when not happy. We learn our first language by the time we are around three years old and generally get better at that language as we use it to communicate. We even learn to write it and read it so we do not have to make the sounds.

But language is not the main way we communicate. Most communication does not need words. It is **non-verbal.**

What emotions or feelings are shown here?

Some people are good at reading **body language** and can tell whether someone is happy or sad by watching how they sit or stand. Experts in body language can even tell when someone is not telling the truth by observing their body language.

Activity 1

Next time you are in a crowded place, take a minute to observe the body language around you. Two people may be in a conversation. If they are interested in what the other person is saying, they lean forward and nod in agreement or shake their head in disbelief.

Active listening is about being involved, really listening and asking questions. If someone is leaning away from the other person or looking bored, they are not really interested. You may even notice this in class! Active listeners check out what they have heard. They may ask a question to clarify a point or may nod encouragement to the speaker.

Facial expressions tell us what people are thinking even when they do not realise it. A smile can be real or pretend. Real smiles include the eyes. A pretend smile is just the mouth stretched to a smile. Sometimes a person can seem cold and distant but they may be shy. If you are shy, remember that a smile works wonders anywhere and makes people feel relaxed.

Try it when you go to placement. Even if you are nervous, think of the nicest things you can and think of what makes you happy, then you will find it easy to smile. Once you smile, everyone smiles back and you feel welcome too.

Activity 2

Can you spot a fake smile? Professor Paul Ekman of the University of California and Dr Wallace V. Friesen of the University of Kentucky have worked out how to spot a fake smile. They found that in real smiles the eyebrows dip slightly.

You can read more about this and do a quiz on the BBC website at http://www.bbc.co.uk/science/humanbody.

Touch or contact can be very comforting, but you must be careful how you use this. Someone may be upset and you feel like giving them a hug to comfort them – but they might be a private person and not want to be touched. It is important to ask yourself what the patient wants, not what you want. Sometimes touch can be misunderstood, especially if someone is from a different culture. In some cultures men and women do not touch, even to shake hands.

Sometimes people you care for may be lonely. If they have few friends, they may misunderstand if you hug them and they may think you want to have a close friendship with them. It is always better to maintain a professional approach. You can be supportive in what you say and how you say it without hugging or touching a person. Of course, at times you may have to use touch. A service user who needs help with a wash or a steadying hand to help them sit down may appreciate your help. Always ask first what the service user would like you to do.

One-to-one communication means you are communicating with one person. A lot of the time we communicate in **groups**.

List how many groups you have communicated with today. Here is my list:

- Got up and spoke to the rest of the family at breakfast.
- Took a bus to work and met friends in the bus station.
- Mid morning went to get a snack with two friends.
- Midday I walked into town with friends and did some shopping.
- Evening met friends to plan a holiday together.

Perhaps you work as part of a group in your lessons or communicate with others as part of a group at work placement.

Sometimes we need to communicate in a **formal** way. We may need to speak with less of an accent so that others can understand us. We may need to write a formal letter when applying for a job. We need to use formal communication when we go for an interview.

Sometimes we can be **informal** with friends or people we know well. When is it good to be informal? When should you be formal?

KEY TERMS

Formal means official, proper or correct.

Activity 3

Make two lists – on one write the times you need to be formal, then on the other list write the times you can use informal communication.

There are some examples to start you off:

Formal communication	Informal communication
Speaking at an interview for a job Writing to an official organisation Giving a presentation	Text to friends or community Talking with friends Email to friends Sometimes speaking to a service user you know

You may notice that in the lists we have both verbal (spoken) and non-verbal communication. Remember – non-verbal communication is the way we communicate most often.

Different cultures communicate in very different ways. When greeting someone in France you may be expected to kiss them on the cheek. In India it may be very bad manners to touch the other person at all. Instead you may be greeted by 'namaste' (see photo below). In England someone may shake your hand or raise their hat. In Japan you greet someone with a bow. The person of lower status must bow lower.

Eye contact in Britain is usually expected when people are talking to each other. In India it is good manners to keep your eyes lowered in the presence of someone older or someone who is your boss. This can lead to problems as many people raised in an Eastern culture may feel it is rude to look someone in the eyes, while the Western person they are talking to may think they are rude not to make eye contact.

In Japan it is good manners to leave a little food on the plate. This means your host has fed you so well that you cannot finish the food. In Britain leaving food on the plate may be considered bad manners because you are implying that the food is not good. With so many cultural differences it is amazing that people do manage to bridge the gap and communicate with people from different cultures. Care workers have to be sensitive to cultural differences. If you are not sure, ask the person you are talking to whether there are any differences you need to be aware of.

Sometimes people use signs to communicate. What do these signs mean?

Children need to learn these meanings if they are not to get run over by traffic.

How about these? People who cannot read the language can recognise these symbols.

Someone who cannot speak may use a picture board to communicate. You could use a picture board if you go abroad on holiday and do not speak the language. We sometimes use them in care if a service user cannot speak. Here is an example. Can you guess which meal the picture board opposite may be used for?

Activity 4

Towards P1, P2, M1, D1.
Make a picture board for things you like to do in your leisure time. Try it out on someone in your class. Could they tell what your pictures mean?

Objects of reference are any objects which represent other things. Children may have a teddy bear or comfort blanket which represents comfort and safety. Older people may have family photographs. These objects denote important aspects of their lives. Carers must be aware of the importance of these. A child might feel secure if they have their blanket. An older person may settle better into a care home if they have their photographs. A religious person may have a Bible or Koran or other religious text which means a lot to them. It may signify their cultural identity and sense of who they are.

Objects of reference communicate a lot about a person. A carer must respect such objects as representing important aspects of the person they are caring for. Sometimes objects of reference bring back memories. Older people may remember their childhood better than what happened yesterday. A packet of sweets similar to those they had as a child may help them remember what it was like to be young. Carers can learn a lot about service users by listening to their stories. A person who is suffering from dementia may be helped to communicate by using objects of reference.

Writing is one way to communicate. Once we could communicate only by letter with friends and relatives who lived far away. Now we have many ways to communicate using writing. Which of these might you be able to teach an older person? Which do you think a young person might know already?

Technological aids to communication have developed rapidly. Many older people use email to keep in contact with friends and family who live far away. Many other people use blogs or Facebook to keep in touch with people. The Internet has changed the way people communicate. Someone who is deaf can communicate with friends using email and text messages. People who have visual problems can use computer software to turn their spoken word into written communication.

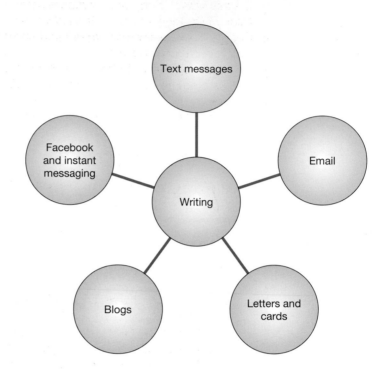

Writing is one way to communicate

If you work with people who have a visual impairment you may discover they use Braille. Those who are visually impaired or losing their sight may also use talking books – recordings of someone reading the book. Famous people who have helped deaf and blind people communicate include Helen Keller and Louis Braille.

Did you know?

According to the RNIB website: on 21 July 2007, *Harry Potter and the Deathly Hallows* was the first novel in the UK to go on sale to the general public in audio, Braille, large print and standard print simultaneously.

Did you know?

Helen Keller was born in America in 1880. At 19 months old she got an infection which left her both deaf and blind. When she was seven years old she had a tutor, Anne Sullivan, who taught her to read and write by spelling each letter into her hand. Helen went on to graduate from university and devoted her life to improving the situation of deaf-blind people.

Did you know?

Braille was invented by Louis Braille in 1829. Louis was blind and invented the system of six raised dots to represent letters. It is still used today. Many documents are produced in Braille as well as text.

Activity 5

Towards P1, P2, M1, D1.
Do this with a friend and compare notes.
Click on to the website of the Royal National Institute for Deaf
People (http://www.rnid.org.uk) and find out what help is available to help
deaf people communicate.
Now click on the website for RNIB (http://www.rnib.org.uk) which supports
people who are blind or partially sighted.

The communication cycle

So what is communication? And how does it happen?

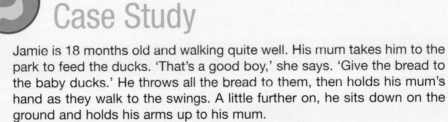

Case Study

Jamie is 18 months old and walking quite well. His mum takes him to the
park to feed the ducks. 'That's a good boy,' she says. 'Give the bread to
the baby ducks.' He throws all the bread to them, then holds his mum's
hand as they walk to the swings. A little further on, he sits down on the
ground and holds his arms up to his mum.

Why do you think he does that?

What is he communicating?

How is he communicating – verbally or without words?

How does his mum communicate with him – verbally or non-verbally?

She picks him up and says, 'You are tired today, aren't you?'

The example of Jamie and his mum shows the different stages of communication.

1 Jamie has the idea – 'I'm tired.'
2 He codes the idea in a way his mum will understand, visually,
   without words.
3 He sends the message by sitting down and lifting up his arms to be
   carried, showing his mum he is tired.
4 She sees what he is doing (receives the message).
5 She decodes the message – he is sitting down because he is tired.
6 She understands he needs to be picked up.

The following diagram shows the stages of communication.

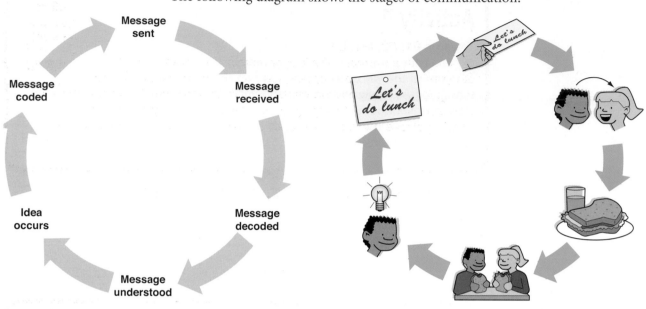

The communication cycle is as follows:

1   Idea occurs.
2   Message coded.
3   Message sent.
4   Message received.
5   Message decoded.
6   Message understood.

Now let's do some practical communication.

Activity 6

Towards P1, P2, M1, D1.
Think of a question you could ask someone in your class.
Perhaps you want to know whether they have heard the latest
music, or you may want to ask whether they have a spare pen. It doesn't
matter what the question is.
Write it down on paper. Give it to the person.
What comes next – Message received or Message decoded or Message
understood?
Hint: what comes last? Check it out with the communication cycle diagram.

What might happen next? Did you think that the cycle would start again? If you asked a question your partner could answer, they would think of the answer, code it in either written or spoken language and send the answer to you. You receive it, read it (or hear it if spoken) and you understand the answer – if you can read their handwriting!

Activity 7

Towards P1, P2, M1, D1.
Try this with a partner – think of something you want them to get you when they go shopping next. Now communicate this to them without using any words. Give them two minutes to get the message. Now ask them what they thought you meant. Did they get it right? Change places and you have to guess what they are asking you to buy for them.

Think back to how you communicated. Which of these did you use?

- Body language
- Facial expression
- Touch or contact.

Was the communication effective? Did it work?

Activity 8

Try another one – line up as a class in birth date order without speaking.

Assuming you did not write down your birth dates, you might have used gestures, nods, smiles, hand signals and eye contact to encode the idea.

2 Examine barriers to effective communication

Sometimes there are problems or barriers to communication. Think back to the activities you just did.

Factors that affect communication may include any of these:

1 Sensory deprivation – if you cannot see very well, you cannot see when people are using non-verbal signals such as a smile or a frown. If you cannot hear very well, you may not be able to hear what someone says in a noisy room.
2 Foreign language – if you speak the same language there are fewer barriers to communication, but just imagine how difficult it is to ask the doctor about your operation if you do not know the language.
3 Jargon is specialist language. It can be a barrier to communication if the person receiving the message does not understand the jargon. A person might feel scared if they are told they have 'plantar fasciitis'. If the doctor says they have 'heel pain' it sounds a lot less scary.
4 Slang or informal language can be a barrier to communication if the other person does not understand the slang. Rhyming slang, like the original East

London slang, uses rhyming words, so 'mince pies' means 'eyes' and 'dog and bone' means 'telephone'. This is fine if the other person knows the same slang but it can be confusing if the other person does not recognise the same terms. 'I tripped on the dog and bone lying on the apples and pears' can sound very strange to someone who does not know what the slang words are. (Did you guess it means 'I tripped on the telephone lying on the stairs'?)

5 Dialect words are used in a local area. In parts of the Midlands, people may use 'y'am' to mean 'you are'. In some parts of Yorkshire, people use 'tha' to mean 'you'. So in the Midlands someone using dialect might say 'Y'am going out?'; in Yorkshire they might say 'Tha'going out?'. Someone who comes from the South of England might have difficulty understanding both of these people.

6 Acronyms are words formed from the initials of other words. EMA, for instance, stands for Education Maintenance Allowance. Perhaps you know what NHS stands for (National Health Service), but how about GP, GSCC or NMC? Acronyms help communication only if everyone knows what they mean, otherwise they actually prevent communication. (GP stands for general practitioner or your local doctor; GSCC stands for General Social Care Council, which registers carers; NMC is the Nursing and Midwifery Council, which registers nurses and midwives.)

Activity 9

Collect as many health and social care-related acronyms as you can and make a poster to remind you what they stand for.

7 Cultural differences can make barriers to communication. We have seen examples of the different meanings of eye contact earlier in the chapter, but did you know that in the Middle East, Asian and Far East cultures the right hand is for clean things and the left hand is for dirty things, such as wiping your bottom? If you are giving out meals to someone from one of these cultures, they may feel unable to eat food if you give it with the left hand. The cultural differences make barriers to communication if they are not understood.

8 Emotions can be barriers to communication. When people are upset or distressed they may not hear what is being said. A person who has just been told that their parent has cancer may not hear that it is a treatable form of cancer because they are so distressed. It is important to make sure that people are able to understand what you are telling them in care. Sometimes they cannot absorb a lot of information at once and need time to adjust.

9 Anxiety can pose similar problems for communication. A person may have been trying for a baby for many years. If they have just been told that there may be a problem with the pregnancy, they may be so anxious that they do not hear what is being said.

10 Both physical and mental disabilities can cause barriers to communication. A person may be physically unable to hear the message, or may have dementia and forget what they have been told.

11 Environmental factors, such as a noisy room or poor lighting, may hamper communication. A person who has problems hearing but usually lip-reads will find this difficult in a darkened room.

12 Sometimes messages are misinterpreted. Nurses in hospital are not allowed to take a verbal prescription over the telephone. The doctor must come to the ward and write the prescription, the dose, the route of administration, how much and how often so that there are no mistakes. It is easy to misinterpret messages and give the right drug in the wrong way. Some drugs are safe to be injected into muscle but can kill if injected into other areas of the body.

13 Humour differs between people and between cultures. What is funny to one person is not necessarily funny to another person. In this country we sometimes make jokes about religion. In many religions this is unacceptable and a person with such beliefs may no longer respect a care worker who jokes about serious matters.

14 Behaviour which is appropriate at home may not be appropriate at work. A family member may benefit from a hug, but a patient may think of it as assault.

15 Aggression of any sort prevents communication. The aggressor communicates only the fact that they are a bully. The victim understands only the fear. It is never acceptable to bully a patient; for example, if they have poor personal hygiene, they will not learn how to be clean from being treated aggressively. They will learn only to hide from the bully. Patients can be aggressive, but this does not help communication. An aggressive patient may be frightened, but the carer will not be able to comfort them if they are themselves in danger of being attacked.

16 Feelings of isolation prevent communication. An isolated or depressed person may not see a smile directed at them or may not pick up on non-verbal communication. Even when a carer talks to them, they may not hear the message if they are deeply depressed.

This list of factors stopping communication seems long, but there are ways of overcoming communication barriers.

Ways to overcome communication barriers

Plenty of light, no background noise

Adapting the environment so there is enough light and there is no background noise will help people lip-read and hear well. Make sure you are directly in front of someone who is trying to lip-read.

Find out what they prefer

Try to understand the person's language needs and preferences and adapt your language to theirs. If someone likes to be called Mrs or Mr, use that term. Do not call them 'dear' or pet names. Use the individual's preferred spoken language. Try to learn the basics of their language so that you can communicate effectively with them.

Listen actively and give them time

Active listening, using appropriate body language, eye contact and nearness or proximity will show the person that you care enough to try to understand them. Allow sufficient time for a patient to communicate with you. If you are in a hurry, tell them when you will be back and when you will be able to listen. Sometimes you do not have time at that moment, but if the patient knows you will return when you say, they may be able to tell you what they are trying to say.

When a person tells you something, check you have understood by repeating the message. When you have given information, get the individual to repeat the message. This saves miscommunication and problems later. You may be getting the name of their GP or their telephone number. Checking it back confirms you have the correct information. If you are sending a patient home, getting them to repeat the instructions you have just given them will ensure they do the right thing when they are at home.

Learn phrases in another language such as BSL

Sometimes other forms of communication are needed. British Sign Language is a specialised language and you may need a signer. This may be arranged through the local branch of the RNID. Signs and pictures may be of use depending on the information to be communicated. Sometimes leaflets are available in other languages, but just because a person speaks a language does not mean they can read it. It is always better to get a translator or interpreter if there is any doubt about how well a person has understood the information they need.

British Sign Language is a specialised language

Use advocates

Sometimes people may speak the language but because of other problems may not be able to express themselves or take in the information they need. They may need an advocate. An advocate speaks on behalf of another and represents their views. Young people sometimes need an advocate if they do not have a family to present their views. People with mental health issues may also need an advocate to help them express their wishes.

According to MIND (http://www.mind.org.uk), the mental health charity, advocacy is a process of supporting and enabling people to:

● express their views and concerns
● access information and services
● defend and promote their rights and responsibilities
● explore choices and options.

Did you know?

Advocacy is often provided by voluntary or charitable organisations which rely on funding from the public. There is a great demand for advocates but it depends where you live whether you will be able to have an advocate if you need one. 'A report by the Social Care Institute for Excellence (SCIE) reveals serious gaps in the provision of advocacy support services for African and Caribbean men – despite their over-representation in the mental health system.' *Source*: http://www.scie.org.uk.

3 Explore diversity and equality in society

Diversity means variety, so diversity in society means variety in society. Here are some ways our society varies.

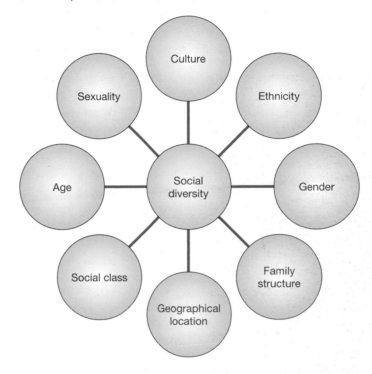

Social factors

Culture

In British society today we have many cultures living alongside each other. Gypsies and travellers originally left India over 1,000 years ago and have lived a nomadic or wandering lifestyle ever since. Travellers have their own culture, or ways of doing things. Often the women would make and sell clothes pegs or lace mats. They would offer to tell fortunes in exchange for a few coins. The men would get work where they could and used to specialise in horse trading. The Gypsy Council, also called the Romany Kris, provides legal advice for travellers because they face discrimination from society. Many councils do not want travellers in their area. As a result of their nomadic lifestyle, travellers get very little health care and find it difficult to get education for the children.

Ethnicity

On 17 March each year the Irish celebrate St Patrick's Day with a parade in Birmingham and London. The Irish are one of the oldest ethnic communities in London. Many came in the 18th and 19th centuries when there was little work in Ireland, but a great need for manual workers in England. They came to help dig the canals and construct the railways. In the 20th century they came to work as nurses

Activity 10

Find out which ethnic groups live in your area. Do they have any special shops or restaurants? Do they work in any particular jobs?

in the NHS. Now Ireland is richer and has plenty of work available, fewer Irish people come to London, but many have settled here permanently and contribute to enriching society.

Another ethnic group which enriches our community is Italians, who have been here for hundreds of years, contributing to the arts and architecture. Italian craftsmen helped decorate some of the grandest houses of England when they were constructed in the 18th century.

Pakistanis came from four main areas of Pakistan and contribute to society by keeping small grocery shops and many Post Offices open. They work long hours for low wages. Many are self-employed and encourage the next generation to get a good education. Some of the second- and third-generation Pakistanis are now members of Parliament, contributing to making society better for all.

The latest ethnic group to arrive in Britain are the Polish. As Britain is a member of the European Union and there is free movement of workers across EU borders, Polish people have arrived to fill the skills gap. They work long hours in jobs such as farming, picking fruit and harvesting vegetables, but earn more than they would in Poland. Recently some have opened shops to sell Polish goods. Most Polish people seem to work very hard.

Gender

In mid-2006 the UK population was estimated at 60 million people, with slightly more females than males. Our society is diverse, or varied, in terms of gender.

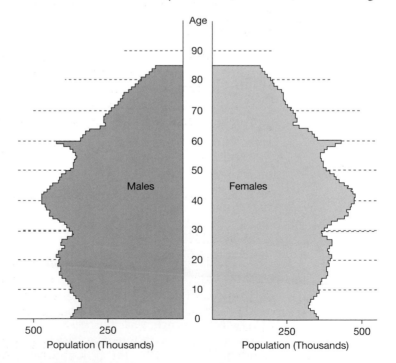

The UK population in 2006
Source: National Statistics website: www.statistics.gov.uk. Crown copyright material is reproduced with the permission of the Controller of HMSO.

Sexuality

Our society is also varied in terms of sexuality or sexual orientation. Some people have partners of the same gender and go through a civil ceremony to make their partnership official. No one has to conform to a set pattern in this society.

Age

Age is yet another way we are a diverse society. People live longer. The fastest-growing age group is the over-80s. It is estimated that more than 9,000 people are over 100 years old in England and Wales, according to the Office of National Statistics. People live longer because of better food, living conditions, hygiene and medical treatment. Women tend to live longer than men; many live alone or in residential accommodation when they are over 85 years old.

Family structures

Family structures have changed. Fewer people now marry. In England and Wales marriages fell by 10 per cent in 2005 (*source*: www.statistics.gov.uk). People who divorce often remarry, so there are people living in non-traditional families. Some families are one parent and one child; other families are two parents and no children. Around 7 out of 10 families are headed by a married couple, but the number of cohabiting parents is rising. The number of families headed by single parents is also increasing.

Activity 11

Jez has a brother. His mum and dad got divorced and then his mum married again. He has two stepsisters now as well as his brother. Sometimes he goes with his brother to visit his dad. Sometimes his sisters go to visit their mum. He has a lot of people to buy birthday presents for. He hardly sees his grandparents on his dad's side now.
What might be the good things about Jez's life? Are there any problems he might have?

Social class

In 2007, Sheffield University researchers found that social class differences are widening in this country (Thomas and Dorling, *Identity in Britain: A cradle-to-grave atlas*). In the poorest parts of the country, young people are far more likely to be out of employment, education and training than in the wealthier parts of the country.

Geographical location

Some of the worst overcrowding in homes occurs in London and Glasgow where families with children may live in flats with no garden. The highest earners live in the areas just outside London. Many areas are separated by wealth. Richer people do not usually live alongside poorer people in this country and most of the wealth is concentrated in the south of England. People in the north tend to be poorer and more likely to be out of work. This shows that while our society has a range of wealth, people do not mix.

Political factors

Role of legislation

Laws tell us how we should behave in society. Legislation is another word for the law. The Employment Equality (Sex Discrimination) Regulations 2005 give men and women the same rights to employment, vocational training, promotion and working conditions. The Children Act 2004 looks at improving children's lives. Services are encouraged to work together to make sure children are cared for properly

The government initiative 'Every Child Matters: Change for Children' aims to improve the services offered to children and young people from birth to age 19. This covers five key areas:

- Be healthy
- Stay safe
- Enjoy and achieve
- Make a positive contribution
- Achieve economic wellbeing.

All organisations providing services to children must now work together through children's trusts. They must share information to protect children from harm and to help them achieve their potential. Young people will have a say in how services are planned and delivered. A Children's Commissioner for England was appointed in 2005 and more commissioners are planned for the other UK countries. The Commissioner's role is to listen to young people and represent their views in public life. 'Every Child Matters' puts into practice the ideas set out in the Children's Act 2004. You can find out more on http://www.everychildmatters.gov.uk.

The 1976 Race Relations Act made racial discrimination illegal. The Race Relations (Amendment) 2000 says that schools, local authorities and hospitals must all get rid of unlawful racial discrimination and promote equality of opportunity and good relations between people of different racial groups.

The Disability Discrimination Act 2005 gave people with disabilities rights in employment, education, access to goods and facilities and when buying land or property. Standards were set requiring public transport to meet the needs of those with disabilities. This means that the rail service has to provide facilities so that disabled people can travel, such as ramps at stations or help from a guard. Buses now have lower platforms to enable people with disabilities to board. The definition of disability was extended to cover 'hidden' disabilities such as HIV, cancer and multiple sclerosis.

The Data Protection Act 1998 came into force on 1 March 2000 (www.ico.gov.uk). The Act applies to 'personal data', which is data about identifiable living individuals, and covers both personal data held electronically and manual or paper data held in structured files or easily accessible systems. The Data Protection Act gives rights to individuals about whom information is held. It also requires those who record and use 'personal information' to follow the principles of good information handling. These say that data must be accurate, not kept for longer than necessary and must be securely stored.

The Care Standards Act 2000 replaces previous legislation such as the Registered Homes Act 1984 and amendments. The Care Standards Act established a new Commission for Social Care Inspection (CSCI) with powers to register, regulate and inspect:

- domiciliary social care providers
- independent fostering agencies
- residential family centres
- boarding schools
- residential care homes for adults
- nursing homes
- children's homes.

The 2000 Act sets out legally required national minimum standards such as minimum room size. CSCI inspectors can demand to see documents about the running of a home and talk to service users in private about the care they receive.

> **Activity 12**
>
> Find out about the work of the CSCI and read an inspection report for your area at www.csci.org.uk.

Role of policy

Government policy changes with whatever political party is in power. The table below may help you understand this complex subject.

Left wing Old Labour	New Labour	Centre party Liberal Democrats	New Right	Right wing Conservatives
Tax people a lot to pay for free education and health, sickness and unemployment benefits.	Tax people a lot but keep private education and health. If people want to pay for private education or care, they should.	Increase taxes a little but improve state schools and hospitals.	There will always be some that have to be helped, but it should be a mix of private and state care. Lower taxes.	Low taxes but people should buy what they need, so they should pay for health care and education. They should have private savings if they are unemployed. Cut benefits.

If we get a left-wing political party in power, we get more services through the state, for example National Health Service hospitals and clinics. If we get a right-wing party in power, we get lower taxes but we have more spare money to pay for private care.

Activity 13

In your class, hold a debate. One person must speak for each viewpoint, then the rest of the class can take turns expressing their views. After 15 minutes, take a vote on which party you would support.

Welfare state

The welfare state means the system in this country for the following areas.

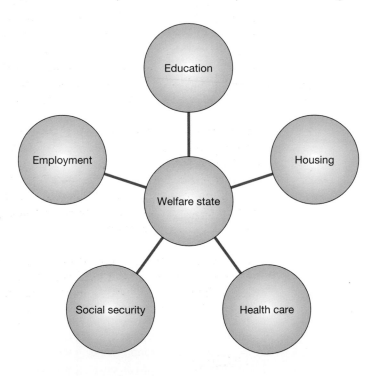

When the Second World War ended in 1945, Britain had lost a lot of houses in the bombing and therefore we had a housing shortage. We also had a shortage of jobs because many of the factories had been used to produce materials for war – now there was no demand for them. Many soldiers returning to Britain were ill or injured. They could not get jobs. People were homeless, hungry and poor. William Beveridge and Nye Bevan, both politicians, introduced the welfare state. This was a plan to fight the five problems of:

- poverty
- idleness

- squalor
- disease
- ignorance.

To combat poverty, they brought in pensions for older people and compulsory contributions for sickness and unemployment benefits. To combat idleness, they set up labour exchanges where people who wanted jobs could register. Employers would then know who was available and could offer them work. To combat squalor, they brought in a planned programme of council housing, building large estates of houses. People who had been bombed out of their homes now had a home rented from the council. To combat disease they set up the National Health Service which was free when people were sick. (They paid for it through taxes.) To combat ignorance, they made education free and compulsory until the age of 15.

The NHS plan

The NHS plan originally provided care from birth through to the end of life, from 'cradle to grave'. As people got healthier they lived longer after they retired. Demand for health care rose. New developments in surgery meant we could now save lives both at the beginning of life – with premature babies surviving – and at the end of life, with people living into their eighties and nineties. In the 1970s many of the heavy industries closed. Coal mining and steel working were lost. Car making was in decline. More and more people were unemployed and needed benefits. Their health suffered because they were depressed.

In the 1980s we could no longer afford free health care. Charges were made for prescriptions, opticians and dentists. Residential care was charged at what it cost the care home instead of being provided free. This was now a mixture of private and public care. It is sometimes called a 'mixed economy of care'. General practitioners were given money and had to buy the care from the cheapest supplier. Sometimes a private hospital could do an operation cheaper than a state hospital and so got the contract for the operation.

The NHS Plan 2000 set out a list of targets to make the NHS more efficient. Targets were set for reducing waiting lists and for reducing illness such as cancer and heart disease. The NHS reforms aim to make the state sector as efficient as the private sector of health care.

Equality

Equality means fairness, giving equal opportunities to everyone in society.

Non-discriminatory practice is practice which does not discriminate. An example of non-discriminatory practice is when care is offered to all those who need it. Babies and children need immunisation to protect them from mumps, measles and rubella. Non-discriminatory practice offers immunisation to all children.

Activity 14

What other types of care are 'non-discriminatory'?
Make your own list, then share your list with a partner. Then work as a group of four and share your lists. Repeat until all the class has a shared list.

Discriminatory practice makes distinctions between who can have care and who cannot. In Scotland residential care is free; in England people have to pay. This is discriminatory practice, based on where a person lives.

Discrimination or making a distinction between people is often based on age, ethnicity, religion, nationality or a person's gender or sexuality. Most of these types of discrimination are illegal in this country. It is not legal to refuse a person treatment because they are too old.

Stereotyping means typecasting or putting people into a category. People are often stereotyped by age, skin colour, gender or religion.

Activity 15

Towards P3 and M2.
Draw a picture of you in the middle of a piece of paper. Now write around the picture all the things that make you who you are. You may have red hair, a gap in your front teeth. You may be small or tall, rounded or slender. What culture do you think you belong to? What do you see as your ethnicity? Are you male or female? How old are you? What type of family do you live in – a single-parent family or one with both parents?

Think of your family – are you a sister or a brother, an aunt or uncle? What do people in your family do for a living? Where do you live?

Continue until you have no space left to write all the things that make you the person you are. Try to decide one category which describes you.

Is it possible to get a true picture of the real you if you are in one category? Most likely you find that a category shows only one part of you – not the whole person.

Which factors contribute to diversity and influence the equality of individuals in society?

Look back at the section if you are not sure.

What are the effects of gender, social class, ethnicity, culture, family structure and age on the equality of individuals in society?

It is difficult to see the whole person if we stereotype them. Labelling someone allows you to see only one aspect of them, not the whole person.

Case Study

Mr A is known as the 'nice old man' in Appleside Care Home. But he is also a grandfather to Tom and father to Michael A. He is a retired headmaster and Mr A the geography teacher to several of the local people. To his local bowling club he is the club secretary.

Why do you think it is not a good idea to label someone?

Did you know?

Many young people who sleep rough have run away from homes where they were being abused. Sometimes the people you would expect to care for them are the people who hurt them. Sometimes the street is safer than their own home.

Often people prejudge a person by how they look. Someone dressed smartly may make a good first impression. Someone dressed casually with uncombed hair may make a poor first impression. Prejudging people can lead to mistakes. The smartly dressed person may be a swindler. The casually dressed person may be a multimillionaire who runs their own company. Prejudice is often based on snap judgements and fear of the unknown. It is better not to make judgements about others – you can never know the full story.

4 Investigate how the principles of the care value base can be used to promote the rights of individuals and significant others

There are three main care values, as illustrated in the diagram below.

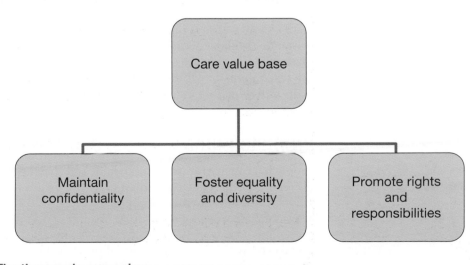

The three main care values

Maintain confidentiality

This means not giving information to anyone who does not have the right to that information. There are a few exceptions when you can break confidentiality:

- when the person is a risk to themselves
- when the person is a risk to others
- if they are at risk from abuse.

Confidentiality can be maintained by:

- not talking to or about service users in a public place
- making sure records are marked 'confidential'
- ensuring records are read only by those who should read them
- ensuring that computer records have passwords.

Confidentiality is important as it builds trust between service users and staff members and can protect them. The principles of confidentiality should be reflected in policies, procedures and guidelines.

Foster equality and diversity

This means understanding the effects on service users of prejudice, stereotyping and labelling. Equality means giving people the same chances. It is not 'treating people exactly the same'.

Here's an example. Jay likes kippers for breakfast. He thinks treating people equally is treating everyone the same, so he makes sure every resident in the care home gets kippers for breakfast. How would you feel if you had to have kippers every morning for breakfast? What could Jay have done to make sure he was really treating people equally?

He could have asked them what they wanted. This is giving people equal chances.

Diversity means difference

Look back to the exercise where you made a picture about you. Compare your pictures and words about you with a partner. How many differences are there? Now compare it with someone else's picture. See how much diversity there is already. This diversity makes life interesting. You can learn new things from other people and you can teach them new things too. Respecting diversity ensures that everyone is treated as an individual.

Promote rights and responsibilities

People have many rights within health and social care. These include the right to be different, to have choice and dignity within health and social care and to be safe and secure. Care workers must support these rights, but they also have their own rights. These include working in a safe environment and not being subjected to abuse. The care value base is just that – basic values in care. It is embedded in all health and social care work. It is in the codes of practice, policies, charters and the expectations of people receiving the service.

Individual rights or entitlements

These include rights to be:

- respected
- treated equally and not discriminated against
- treated as an individual
- treated in a dignified way
- allowed privacy
- protected from danger and harm
- allowed access to information about oneself
- able to communicate using one's preferred methods of communication and language
- cared for in a way that meets one's needs, takes account of one's choices and protects them.

Activity 16

Towards P4, P5, M3, D2.
Read the case study below and make a list of what rights have been ignored. Then compare notes with a partner.

Case Study

Sheila works in a care home for older people with dementia. She sees Carla, another assistant, dress Mr Phillips. Carla chooses the clothes that he should wear without consulting Mr Phillips.

After he is dressed Mr Phillips comes down for his breakfast. He is a strict orthodox Jew. The new care assistant Tina is giving Mr Phillips his breakfast and has not been told about any dietary needs that Mr Phillips has. She offers him a choice of bacon and eggs or sausage and tomatoes. He says he is not hungry. Mr Phillips requests a visit to the synagogue but this is refused as there are no staff to take him.

Carla, Tina and Sheila then write up the notes from the shift. Sheila finishes her section and leaves Carla and Tina to finish their sections. Carla and Tina forget to put their notes away and are still talking about Mr Phillips when they go for a drink after work.

Did you notice any of these?

- Lack of respect for his wishes.
- He was not treated equally as he was not offered any food he could eat.
- He was discriminated against because his spiritual needs were not considered.
- He was not treated as an individual but had to fit in with the routines.
- He was not treated in a dignified way. It is almost as though he does not matter.

We do not know whether he has his privacy, but certainly his confidentiality was not respected because the staff talked about him outside the home. He was not really cared for in a way that meets his needs or offers him choice. Hopefully you will not see such poor practice in any care setting.

Workers' responsibilities

People who work in care have a duty to actively support patients and service users to express their needs, views and preferences. They should use the patient's preferred method of communication and not make the patient adapt to them.

Care workers must promote equality of opportunity, giving the same chances to all. They must maintain confidentiality and disclose information only where there is a risk to the service user or to others or where there is a risk of abuse. Care workers must balance rights and responsibilities.

Activity 17

Towards P4, P5, M3, D2.
See the case study below and try to decide whose rights are involved

Case Study

David lives with three other people in sheltered housing. Two care workers are on duty at all times. David likes to go to the shop but cannot go alone as he gets lost. One day he decides he wants to go to the shop, but Tim, his carer, is on duty with a new member of staff. If Tim takes David to the shop, the new carer would be left with three service users and might not be able to manage. If Tim asks the new carer to take David, the carer might not be able to manage the situation if David panics and gets aggressive.

Did you think David's rights were involved? Yes, they were. Other residents also had rights to be with a member of staff who knew what to do. The new member of staff also had rights not to be asked to do something they were unsure about.

Sometimes it is difficult to respect everyone's rights. In this case, a compromise was reached and they all went to the shop together, which they enjoyed. Two carers could safely manage the situation, so no one was at risk.

Recording, storing and retrieving information is a very important responsibility for carers. Care workers must understand the importance of accurate recording, storing and retrieving of information.

Here's an example. Mr F has tablets for his heart. Why do you think it is important that the nurse signs every time she has given the tablets? Why is it important that the drug sheet is kept safely where other nurses can find it?

Did you guess what might happen if the nurse did not sign?

● Someone else could give the tablets again, thinking they had been forgotten. Mr F would then have had a double dose and might be very ill because of it.
● If the drug chart was not safely stored, it might have been thrown away by accident.
● If it was lost, the next nurse on duty might not have realised that Mr F needed tablets.

SUMMARY

● **In this chapter we have looked at the following:**

Communication

● **How to communicate verbally and non-verbally, both in groups and in one-to-one situations.**
● **Formal and informal communication.**
● **Cultural differences in communication.**
● **The communication cycle.**
● **Barriers to communication and how to overcome them.**

Diversity and equality in society

● **Social factors**   ● **Ethnicity**
● **Gender**   ● **Age**
● **Family structure**   ● **Social class**
● **Political factors**   ● **Legislation**
● **The role of policy**   ● **The welfare state**
● **The NHS plan**   ● **Equality**
● **Discriminatory and non-discriminatory practice**

The care value base and how it can help carers:

● **maintain confidentiality**
● **encourage equality and diversity**
● **promote rights and responsibilities**
● **ensure individuals have their rights respected**
● **know their responsibilities.**

Grading grid

In order to pass this unit, the evidence that the learner presents for assessment needs to demonstrate that they can meet all of the learning outcomes for the unit. The criteria for a pass grade describe the level of achievement required to pass this unit.

Grading criteria

To achieve a pass grade the evidence must show that the learner is able to:	To achieve a merit grade the evidence must show that, in addition to the pass criteria, the learner is able to:	To achieve a distinction grade the evidence must show that, in addition to the pass and merit criteria, the learner is able to:
P1 participate in one one-to-one interaction and one group interaction and identify the communication skills that contributed to their success	**M1** describe the interactions and suggest additional skills or factors that would have improved communication	**D1** explain how communication skills can be used in a health or social care environment to assist effective communication
P2 identify potential barriers to effective communication and suggest examples of how they can be overcome	**M2** describe the effects of at least six factors on the equality of individuals in society	**D2** explain how the principles of the care value base and care workers' responsibilities can be applied to promoting patients'/service users' rights
P3 identify the factors that contribute to diversity and influence the equality of individuals in society	**M3** use examples to describe how the principles of the care value base and care workers' responsibilities promote patients'/service users' rights	
P4 describe the rights of patients/service users		
P5 identify the principles of the care value base and care workers' responsibilities to patients/service users		

As individuals we all have different physical, intellectual, emotional and social needs. Understanding the individual needs of people is fundamental within health and social care. In this unit we will look at the different needs that individuals might have and also the different life choices which people make. We will examine the factors and life choices which influence different health needs. We will also look at maintaining health and safety within health and social care settings.

Learning Outcomes

On completion of this unit you should be able to:

1. Explore the everyday needs of individuals in society
2. Examine factors that influence the health and needs of individuals
3. Investigate potential hazards in health and social care environments
4. Examine the main principles of health and safety legislation and guidelines for health and social care environments.

1 Explore the everyday needs of individuals in society

Every individual person has individual needs within society. These needs can be considered in categories such as *physical, intellectual, emotional* and *social*. Or they can be categorised in terms of a ladder of needs.

Activity 1

What do we really need to survive? Make a list of everything that is essential to survive within society. Remember that what you would like is not necessarily the same as what you need!

The needs of people within society

Things that people need can be considered in terms of PIES. This stands for:

● **Physical** needs – these relate to the body, e.g. food, shelter, water
● **Intellectual** needs – these are about stimulating the brain, e.g. going to college, doing crosswords, attending an evening class or reading a book – these are all activities that involve the brain

- **Emotional** needs – these are about belonging, having a sense of wellbeing and self-esteem. They also relate to being able to handle emotions appropriately, e.g. frustration or anger
- **Social** needs – these are about having and maintaining supportive relationships, friendships and a place in society.

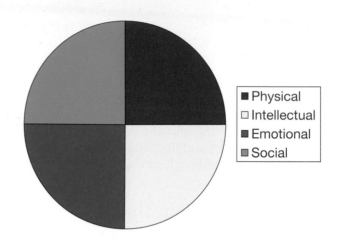

The PIES piechart.

Activity 2

Read the following case studies.

Case Studies

David is a 65-year-old widowed man. He smokes 15 cigarettes a day. He is a member of a walking club and attends the club's walking and social events. He also reads regularly and has some good supportive friends.

His daughter Sharon is 30 and married with two small children. Her husband works away from home a lot and Dad (David) lives a three-hour drive away. She regularly finds herself exhausted and has little time for herself. Although her children eat a healthy diet, Sharon finds she snacks on chocolate and ready meals.

Sharon's friend Stacey works long hours and as a result she has little time for herself. She has recently moved into a new area and does not know many people. She eats a healthy diet and exercises on a regular basis.

Activity 2 (continued)

1 Identify the physical, intellectual, emotional and social factors of each of the individuals in each of the case studies.
2 What are they doing that is good for their health?
3 What are they doing that may harm their health?
4 What would you recommend they do to improve their health?

Maslow's Hierarchy of Needs

In 1943, the psychologist Abraham Maslow developed a 'Hierarchy of Needs' which he showed in a pyramid with different levels.

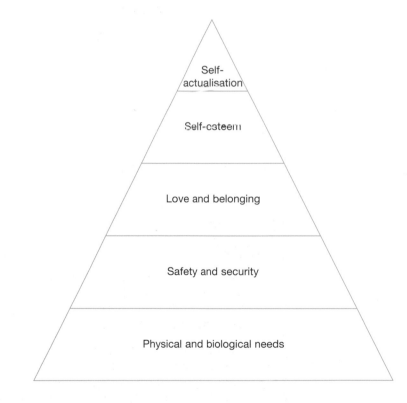

Maslow's Hierarchy of Needs

Maslow argued that everyone has basic needs that must be met. These basic needs are on the first rung of the hierarchy or ladder. Once these needs are met the person can progress onto the next level. However, if the basic needs are not met, these will become the priority. At the highest level is the level of 'self-actualisation'. This is when the individual is displaying and using their full potential.

As Maslow's Hierarchy of Needs shows, human beings yearn for much more than just the basics. The lower levels are about food and shelter, warmth and safety, and the higher needs are about self-esteem, self-worth, creativity and feeling fulfilled as an individual.

2 Examine factors that influence the health and needs of individuals

There are many different factors which can influence the health and needs of individuals. These may be physical factors, lifestyle factors or socio-economic factors.

Physical factors

Biological inheritance is about the genes that are passed down from your parents. Sometimes this genetic make-up can cause genetically inherited conditions such as Down's Syndrome or Cystic Fibrosis. These conditions have an impact upon the health and needs of people.

Down's Syndrome

Down's Syndrome is caused by the genetic make-up of an individual. People with Down's Syndrome often have a number of noticeable features. These may include a flat facial profile, a small mouth which can make the tongue appear slightly larger, and broader hands with shorter fingers (*source*: www.downsyndrome.org.uk). They may have medical conditions, such as heart problems, sight or hearing problems. They will also have some degree of learning disability. Therefore having Down's Syndrome is likely to impact on that individual's physical, intellectual, emotional and social needs. People with Down's Syndrome will need extra support and care throughout their lives.

Activity 3

Look at the following genetic conditions: PKU, cystic fibrosis, sickle cell anaemia, progeria.

- What are they?
- How are they treated?
- How might each of these conditions impact upon the health and needs of the individuals?

Environment

The environment is made up of all the surrounding influences that impact on our lives and this can include pollution. Pollution may be in terms of air, light, water or noise. These kinds of pollution can have a number of effects on the health and needs of people. For example, air pollution has been linked to breathing difficulties and it may aggravate asthma in certain people. Noise pollution can impact upon people socially: what do you think it might be like living next to very noisy and disruptive neighbours? Noise pollution can be so extreme as to affect people's emotional wellbeing and physical health – for example if it causes stress, lack of sleep and anxiety.

Activity 4

Using the Internet, look for newspaper articles or news stories on different kinds of pollution and the effects they might have (the BBC website www.bbc.co.uk/news is a good source). What are some of the implications for health listed within these articles? Can you think of anything else?

Lifestyle factors

Lifestyle factors are those factors about which we have a choice – we can choose whether or not we indulge in them. These could include drinking alcohol, taking illegal or legal drugs, smoking and sexual practices.

Substance abuse

Alcohol abuse can impact upon a person's health and wellbeing. As different types of drinks have different amounts of alcohol, we use a system of units to compare the amount of alcohol within them. For example, a small glass of wine is around 1 unit whereas a pint of standard-strength beer tends to be around 2 units. The current Department of Health guidelines state that women should drink no more than 2–3 units of alcohol per day and men should drink no more than 4–5 units per day. However, statistics show that many people in the UK do not stick to these guidelines.

Over-consumption of alcohol can have serious implications for a person's health. Statistics from the NHS show that around half of pedestrians (aged 16–60) killed in road accidents have more alcohol in their system than the legal drink-drive limit. Statistics also show that around 1,000 children under the age of 15 are admitted to hospital each year needing emergency treatment due to alcohol poisoning.

In the short term, drinking too much alcohol can lead to blurred eyesight, slurred speech, loss of balance, nausea and vomiting – this is what is meant by 'being drunk'. Alcohol can also affect your reactions and your judgement, causing heightened emotions or loss of inhibitions. Due to the high sugar content and alcohol being a diuretic (it increases the rate of urination), alcohol causes dehydration and headaches. If someone continues to consume an excessive amount of alcohol there can be many long-term consequences. Alcohol itself is a depressant drug and can

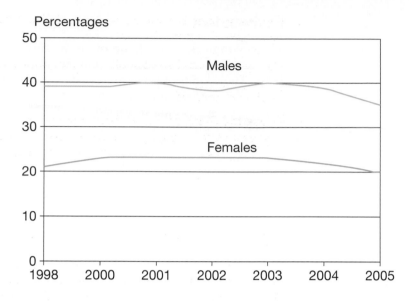

Percentages

Adults exceeding recommended daily benchmarks of alcohol on at least one day during the last week: by sex, Great Britain.
Source: Social Trends. National Statistics website: www.statistics.gov.uk. Crown copyright material is reproduced with the permission of the Controller of HMSO.

affect people in different ways: some may just 'feel down' but others may suffer severe depression. The Department of Health links 25,000 deaths each year to alcohol. Long-term alcohol abuse can lead to liver disease (cirrhosis), heart failure, brain damage, high blood pressure, as well as various types of cancer. For more information go to the Alcohol Concern website at www.alcoholconcern.org.uk.

There are also social and economic factors involved in the excessive consumption of alcohol. Can you think of some of these factors? For example:

- How would it impact on family and friends?
- What about the person's job?
- And what economic impact could it have?

Drugs

There is a wide range of drugs – some are legal and some are illegal. We can all think of **legal drugs**, for example paracetamol and ibuprofen can be bought in a shop or pharmacy. Used in small quantities, they should not cause harm. However, using **illegal drugs** can have serious implications – not only can they impact on an individual's health and wellbeing but their use can lead to prosecution.

Drugs can be divided into different categories: stimulants and depressants. Stimulants increase activity in the brain. Some examples of stimulants are tobacco or ecstasy. Depressants, meanwhile, decrease activity in the brain. Alcohol is in this category. Drugs may also be hallucinogens – these alter the way a person sees or hears things. Hallucinogenic drugs include cannabis, magic mushrooms and LSD. Drugs which have a painkilling effect are known as analgesics – such as heroin. Some drugs, such as cocaine, may have a stimulant effect at first, then cause depression later. For some people, alcohol also has this effect. As you can see, people respond to drugs in different ways.

Activity 5

Use the websites www.talktofrank.com or www.mindbodysoul.gov.uk to choose one illegal drug to research. Look at the implications for health and wellbeing and present this information in a leaflet.

Personal hygiene

Poor or inadequate personal hygiene can impact upon a person's health and their needs. It can have physical consequences – for example, bacteria and fungus on the skin that are not washed off can lead to acne, body odour or athlete's foot. There may also be social consequences – people may not want to be friends with that person. This in turn can impact upon a person's emotional health and wellbeing.

Smoking

Smoking can cause many health problems. Tobacco smoke itself contains over 4,000 chemicals. The three main chemicals found in cigarettes are tar, carbon monoxide and nicotine.

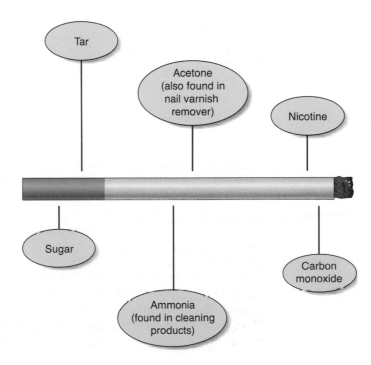

- **Tar** causes yellowish-brown staining of fingers, teeth and lungs. Around 70 per cent of the tar from smoke remains in the lungs. The tar also destroys the cilia (small hairs) in the lungs, which are responsible for protecting the lungs from infection and dirt and keeping the lungs clean and clear (hence the smoker's cough). Tar also narrows the bronchioles and is linked to several different cancers, as explained below.
- **Carbon monoxide** is a poisonous gas. It stops the blood taking up oxygen from the lungs. The body needs a good level of oxygen in the bloodstream to function well. Therefore carbon monoxide cuts down the efficiency of the lungs.
- **Nicotine** is the addictive substance in a cigarette. Nicotine goes into the bloodstream and reaches the brain around 7–10 seconds later. Nicotine also raises blood pressure and heart rate. Smokers become dependent on cigarettes because of this highly addictive chemical. (*Source*: www.nhs.uk)

The effects of smoking on the body

Around one in four British adults smokes. According to Cancer Research UK, men are still more likely to smoke than women – 27 per cent of men and 25 per cent of women smoke.

Smoking causes fingers and teeth to become stained, hair, breath and clothes to smell and can cause your skin to dry out. If someone continues to smoke there are many serious effects on the body. The habit can cause cancers, especially of the lung, mouth or throat. It can lead to chronic bronchitis or emphysema and can affect breathing and circulation. The most common conditions caused by smoking are coronary heart disease, lung cancer, bronchitis, emphysema and pneumonia (*source*: NHS).

Cancer

Smoking is a big risk factor for many types of cancer. Cancer Research UK states that tobacco is the cause of 90 per cent of lung cancers, and 29 per cent of all cancers are linked to smoking (*source*: http://www.cancerhelp.org.uk/help/default.asp?page=3823). Smoking can increase your risk of developing cancers in other parts of the body such as the mouth, nose, stomach and larynx (voicebox).

Coronary heart disease

Smoking increases the risk of coronary heart disease. The British Heart Foundation found that mortality from coronary heart disease is around 60 per cent higher in smokers than in non-smokers (*source*: http://www.heartstats.org/topic.asp?id=876). Smoking can also cause problems such as atherosclerosis, which is a build-up of substances in the arteries. Smokers can be more prone to heart attacks.

Emphysema

Smokers are at an increased risk of suffering from the serious lung condition emphysema which can cause severe breathing problems. Although it can start simply as breathlessness during exercise and a persistent cough, emphysema can leave people housebound and reliant on oxygen supplies and can eventually contribute to death.

There are also many dangers from second-hand smoke. This can cause problems in the short term such as irritation of the eyes, problems breathing or asthma or throat troubles. Longer term it can cause a higher risk of developing lung cancer and other smoking-related illnesses. Doctors estimate that second-hand smoke kills more than 600 people a year in the UK.

Activity 6

Instigate a class discussion. What do you think about the smoking ban which came into effect in England on 1 July 2007? (Scotland, Wales and Northern Ireland already had similar smoking bans in place.) The government hopes it will help smokers to quit and discourage children from taking up the habit. Do you think the smoking ban will work?

Diet

A healthy diet is one which is balanced. It should contain foods from all five food groups.

The balance of good health

The five main food groups are as follows:

- Fruit and vegetables. These contain a variety of nutrients such as fibre, vitamins and minerals.
- Bread, cereal and potatoes. These provide energy as they contain carbohydrates and fibre.
- Dairy and milk products, including yoghurt and cheese.

- Meat, fish and alternatives. These provide us with protein which is essential for growth and repair.
- Fats and foods containing sugars. These should be eaten in small amounts.

Eating too much or too little of a particular food group can have consequences for health. There are many benefits in eating a healthy diet. It can help improve concentration and increase energy and it can also prevent diseases such as 'a third of all cancers, diabetes, osteoporosis (thinning bones), heart disease, strokes and tooth decay, as well as many other diet-related conditions' (*source*: http://www. nhsdirect.nhs.uk/articles/article.aspx?articleId=474&sectionId=34).

People who are overweight are at higher risk of suffering a heart attack. High blood pressure is also a risk in an unhealthy diet.

Physical exercise

There are many benefits of physical exercise. These include more energy, reduced stress, stronger bones and muscles, improved sleep and a sense of achievement and enjoyment. Exercise can also help improve health problems such as coronary heart disease and stroke, high blood pressure, obesity or stress. Exercise can benefit mental and physical wellbeing. Have a look at the information on Keeping Your Heart Healthy and Staying Active on the British Heart Foundation's website at www.bhf.org.uk.

Stress

People can become stressed for a variety of reasons. These may include personal issues (emotional or financial worries) or work-related issues. There are a number of consequences of stress, including headaches, tiredness and anxiety in the short term and an increased risk of heart disease, depression or stomach ulcers in the long term.

Activity 7

What are the most common sources of stress nowadays? Think of some ways in which an individual can reduce their stress levels. Present this information in a leaflet.

Sexual practices

Unsafe sexual practices can have a range of consequences for an individual's health and wellbeing. These consequences could include unwanted pregnancy or sexually transmitted infections (STIs).

Contraception

Contraception gives choice over when (and if) you choose to have a baby. No method is 100 per cent effective and only some methods prevent against STIs. Some of the methods are shown below.

Barrier	Hormonal	Mechanical	Surgical
Diaphragm	The 'pill'	Intrauterine devices	Sterilisation
Condoms	Injections		
Surgical caps	Implants		

(*Source:* www.nhsdirect.nhs.uk)

Barrier methods

These methods work by stopping sperm from reaching the egg to fertilise it. There are both male and female condoms, although the male condom is much more commonly used. For men, the male condom covers the penis. For women, the female condom lines the vagina. Condoms can also provide protection against STIs. Diaphragms and caps are dome-shaped discs which cover the cervix.

Hormonal methods

This type of contraception can be injected or taken by mouth. Implants can also be given. This method has an effect on the hormonal levels of a woman to stop her becoming pregnant. There are two types of contraceptive pill – the combined pill and the progesterone-only pill. The combined pill contains both oestrogen and progesterone. The effect of these is to stop eggs being released from the ovaries. The progesterone-only pill causes mucus at the neck of the womb to thicken which makes it harder for sperm to penetrate. Alternatively, injections of progesterone can be given (about every 12 weeks) or a small implant can be placed in the upper arm. These work by releasing a dose of progesterone into the body.

Mechanical methods

Intrauterine devices (IUD) are also known as coils. The IUD is inserted into the womb and prevents sperm from penetrating the egg. It causes an increase of white blood cells into the cervix that kill the sperm.

Surgical methods

This is an operation on either a woman or a man, which causes them to become infertile. It should be used only when you are sure you no longer want more children, since it is not always reversible.

Sexually transmitted infections (STIs)

There are many examples of sexually transmitted infections. Some are listed below (*source*: www.bupa.com).

Chlamydia

This is the most common STI and is a bacterial infection. Often, women with chlamydia will have no symptoms, or only mild ones. It has been estimated that chlamydia affects up to one in ten women, with 75 per cent showing no symptoms at all. For women, possible symptoms include lower abdominal pain, bleeding between periods or unusual vaginal discharge. For men, symptoms include discharge from the penis or pain on passing urine. Chlamydia is serious, as it can cause long-term pelvic pain or even infertility if it is not treated, but it can be treated quite easily with antibiotics. There are now self-testing kits which can be bought for home testing.

Pubic lice

Pubic lice may live in pubic or other body hair. They lay eggs that stick to the hairs and this can cause itching and inflammation. This can be treated with lotions and special shampoos.

Gonorrhoea

This is also a bacterial infection. For women, symptoms may include an increase in vaginal discharge and pain on passing urine. Men may have a discharge. Again, there may not be any symptoms. If it is not treated, gonorrhoea can lead to pelvic inflammatory disease, infections, inflammations and infertility in both men and women. It can be treated with antibiotics.

HIV and AIDS

AIDS (Acquired Immune Deficiency Syndrome) is a disease of the immune system which is caused by HIV (Human Immunodeficiency Syndrome). HIV can attack the immune system, meaning that a person cannot fight off infections. This causes the immune system to become weaker. It is infectious and can be passed on through unprotected sex.

There is currently no cure for AIDS, although drugs can be taken which slow down the progress of the disease. AIDS is diagnosed through a blood test. For more information go the Terrence Higgins Trust (http://www.tht.org.uk/), an HIV and AIDS charity.

There are many different forms of contraception available, although only condoms can prevent against STIs. As we have seen, STIs can have a range of short- and long-term consequences. The most important thing to remember is that early detection is the key to successful treatment.

Socio-economic factors

Accessibility to services

How accessible a service is can impact on the health and needs of individuals. This accessibility can be for a number of reasons. It could be to do with the services within the local area, or that barriers exist which stop individuals from accessing a service. These barriers could be financial, social or cultural reasons or from individual preferences. For more information see *Unit 8: Health and Social Care Services*, page 191. If an individual cannot access services, then this may result in their health problems getting worse or not being treated.

Education

A positive experience of education can benefit an individual. It can lead to a sense of achievement and wellbeing and can increase a person's job prospects in later life. Education may also have some impact on health and wellbeing. Deadlines or exam time can be a source of stress. People may experience bullying, which can negatively impact upon their self-esteem and wellbeing. Conversely, a lack of education can negatively impact upon someone's achievement. It may also damage their job prospects and financial prospects in later life.

Housing

Poor housing can have a number of implications for health and wellbeing. For example, poor quality housing can impact emotionally upon a person's self-esteem. Socially it may mean that you would feel less inclined to invite friends round. Physically, housing can also have negative impacts on health and wellbeing. Damp housing can lead to an increase in asthma or other breathing difficulties such as bronchitis. Older people and the very young may be at risk of ill-health from damp or draughty housing. The Acheson Report (1999), which was an inquiry into health inequalities, found that those in temporary accommodation had a higher rate of accidents.

Income

A good income can have a positive impact, as it means that money is available to buy items for a healthy lifestyle, or luxury goods. Having a low income can be a major source of stress and worry, and can prevent people from buying healthy or essential items. Again the Acheson Report links income and health.

Media

The media can have an influence upon what you buy and what you think. This can be positive, such as information about health promotion. However, the media can also have a negative influence. There is an ongoing debate about the negative impact of media on body image, for example, and this has been linked to an increase in eating disorders. For more information on eating disorders go to The National Centre for Eating Disorders website at http://www.eating-disorders.org.uk/info.htm.

Religion and culture

Religion and culture can impact upon a number of factors to do with health and wellbeing. For example, certain religions may impact upon care needs or the food you eat – Muslims will not eat pork and people who are Christian may want to celebrate on a Sunday. Culture can impact upon health and needs in terms of beliefs and attitudes towards health and wellbeing.

Employment

Employment can have an impact upon the health and needs of people. Positively, employment provides a source of income which impacts upon a person's ability to purchase goods. Employment can also give an individual a sense of value and self-worth which can increase their self-esteem and wellbeing. On the negative side, employment can make individuals feel stressed, which can negatively impact upon their health and wellbeing. Employment which does not value a person, or undermines them, can negatively impact on their self-esteem.

Gender

Being male or female can impact upon health and wellbeing. The 2001 Census asked about people's experiences of health. Overall a greater proportion of men than women experienced good health (*source*: Social Trends London: TSO No. 34 2004 edition, editors: Carol Summerfield and Penny Babb). Nevertheless, in the UK life expectancy for women is higher than for men.

Social class

Social class is a way of dividing up the population – for example, by classifying them by the jobs they do. Which social class a person falls into can impact upon their health and wellbeing.

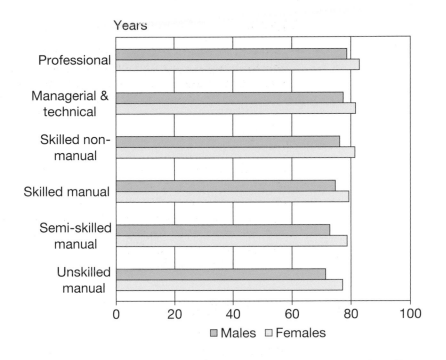

Years

A person's social class can have implications for their health and needs. This graph shows that those in the lower social classes will die earlier than those in the higher social classes. Self-reporting of poor health is also lowest among those in the higher social classes.

Abuse

When working in health and social care it is important for the wellbeing of the service users to be aware of signs and symptoms of abuse and to know what to do if you have suspicions. Vulnerable people are especially prone to abuse. This includes children, older people and those with physical and learning disabilities. Abuse can take many forms, including physical, emotional, sexual, mental or social.

The NSPCC defines **physical** abuse as including hitting, shaking, kicking, punching, scalding, suffocating and other ways of inflicting pain or injury to a child or other individual; **emotional** abuse as when a parent or carer behaves in a way that is likely to seriously affect their child's emotional development; **sexual** abuse as forcing or tricking a child or other individual into taking part in any kind of sexual activity (*source*: www.nspcc.org.uk).

Abuse could also be **financial**, which may include using a person's money without their knowledge or understanding, or theft of an individual's money and possessions. Abuse can take the form of **neglect**, which means depriving a vulnerable person of what they need, such as food, warmth, medication or activities.

There are different reasons as to why abuse may occur. This may be due to someone trying to take power and control, so it is intentional abuse, or it could be unintentional abuse such as work-related issues, exhaustion or stress because of the way in which an organisation is run. People may also be unaware of the effect they are having on someone else.

Possible signs of abuse

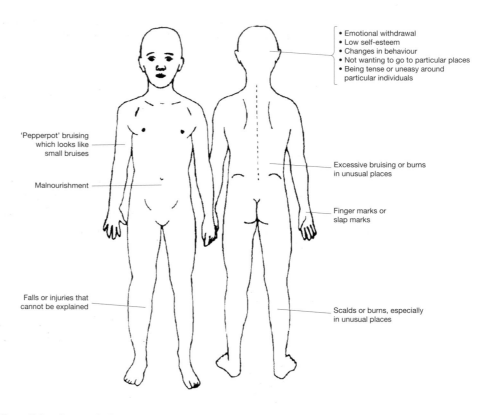

- Emotional withdrawal
- Low self-esteem
- Changes in behaviour
- Not wanting to go to particular places
- Being tense or uneasy around particular individuals

'Pepperpot' bruising which looks like small bruises

Malnourishment

Excessive bruising or burns in unusual places

Finger marks or slap marks

Falls or injuries that cannot be explained

Scalds or burns, especially in unusual places

Possible signs of abuse

KEY TERMS

Disclosure means when someone tells someone else.

What to do: Any suspicion or disclosure of abuse must be taken seriously and be properly looked into. You must report any allegation of abuse to your line manager as soon as possible. You have a legal responsibility to report it. You should also record in writing exactly what the conversation was, rather than rely on your memory. You should not discuss the disclosure with the person who is alleged to be the abuser or with other members of the staff team. You should avoid saying that you 'won't tell anyone' if the person disclosing it asks you. Even though they may be seeking this reassurance from you, withholding the allegation may result in more harm.

Writing the report: When writing your report of the allegation, you should ensure that the information is exactly what the person said to you rather than your interpretation of it. It must be an accurate account and it should also record the time and place of the conversation and any other relevant details.

What happens once an allegation has been made? Each workplace will have its own policies and procedures on addressing allegations of abuse and it is these which will be followed in the event of a disclosure. The allegation should always be taken seriously and investigated thoroughly. Support will be offered to the individual making the allegation and all those involved within the investigation.

Activity 8

Using your work placement, ask them about their abuse policy. Who would you report any allegations to?

All of these factors may have implications in the short term, medium term or long term.

Self-harm

Self-harm is when someone deliberately hurts or injures themselves. It can take a number of forms, including cutting, punching or burning oneself (*source*: www.selfharm.org.uk). Self-harm may be used by the person as a way of dealing with pressure or anxiety. However, professionals such as counsellors and psychologists can help.

Action plan

One way of encouraging an individual to change their lifestyle is to set targets to achieve towards bigger goals. These goals should be SMART:

Specific

Measurable

Accurate

Realistic

Timed.

In other words, the targets should be achievable. For example, it is unrealistic to expect an individual to go from smoking, doing little exercise and eating a poor diet to giving up smoking and running marathons in one week! This is not realistic and not helpful. Therefore, goals should include targets to achieve in the short term (in the next couple of weeks), medium term (in the next month or two) and longer term (over the course of the next 3–4 months or longer).

Look at this example:
John smokes 20 cigarettes a day and does very little exercise. A plan for him could be:

● Short term – cut down to ten cigarettes a day, seek medical assistance for support. Research possible exercise options.

- Medium term – cut down to five cigarettes a day. Try out different exercise options, building up slowly.
- Long term – stop smoking. Continue to exercise on a regular basis.

Activity 9

Choose one of the following and produce an action plan. Remember to include possible sources of help and advice.

- Billy eats an unhealthy diet and drinks 30 units of alcohol a week.
- Julie has few friends and smokes 10 cigarettes a day.
- David has poor personal hygiene and does little exercise.

Remember

A good plan must reflect the personal circumstances of the person. If someone has very little money, then asking them to join a gym will not necessarily be affordable for them. Where else could they go to exercise? You should also consider time constraints and social circumstances. It is useful to provide the individual who is making changes to their health with some supporting material. This could include health promotion leaflets or some information that reminds them how they will benefit from making those changes. Hints and tips or different things to try are also beneficial. However, scare tactics are not particularly helpful – the person who smokes or drinks too much needs support and advice more than just scary statistics. Look at the hints below for John, who wants to cut down on the amount of alcohol he is drinking.

Action plan for John

Aim: Reduce alcohol intake.

- Keep a log or diary of the amount of alcohol you are drinking and how you are feeling at the time.
- Alternate alcoholic drinks with non-alcoholic drinks. (It is a good idea to match every drink with a glass of water.)
- Go to places where alcohol is not served.
- Get support and encouragement from family and friends.
- If necessary, seek professional support too. You could start off by going to see your GP and discussing sources of support with them.

3 Investigate potential hazards in health and social care environments

When working in health and social care environments there are different things that may cause accidents to occur. Look at the picture below of Uneasy Nursery Ltd.

KEY TERMS

A **hazard** is something that can cause harm.

Activity 10

Make a list of the factors that you can identify in the picture of the nursery above which may present a hazard.

Activity 11

For each of the hazards you have identified, explain what may occur as a result of these hazards. (Remember to think of the impact on staff, children, the company and the public as well as service users.)

Responsibilities of employers and employees

When working within health and social care settings, the employer has to provide certain measures to ensure our safety (as staff) and the health and safety of service users. However, as employees we also have a responsibility for the health and safety of ourselves and others.

Activity 12

Make a list of everything that you do at placement that helps maintain health and safety. Or talk to your placement supervisor about what your role is to maintain health and safety in your placement.

Discuss your answers with others in the group.

Employers should	Employees should
Put in place measures to ensure health and safety for all	Co-operate with supervisors and managers on health and safety issues
Consult with employees on health and safety issues	Not mess about with anything provided to help maintain health and safety
Provide information, instruction and support on health and safety issues	Take reasonable care for their own health and safety
Carry out a risk assessment if there are five or more employees	Report any health and safety concerns to an appropriate person
Ensure safe handling and use of substances	

Activity 13

If an accident occurred because of the following, which would be the fault of employers and which would be your fault as an employee?

- You and your friend take turns in lifting each other in the hoist for fun.
- Your employer never asks you about any specific health and safety concerns you may have.
- You do not check the fire alarm as you have been asked to do, but you say that you have done so.
- You leave a cleaning fluid bottle out and a child swallows some of its contents.
- Your employer does not provide training for you.

Reducing risks in health and social care environments

There are various ways in which the risks from these hazards can be reduced. For example, cutting the risk of a fire occurring can be achieved by:

● stopping smoking indoors (now illegal through the Licensing Act 2003)
● having regular plug socket/electrical testing
● supervising all cooking
● avoiding using higher-risk appliances such as chip pans
● clearing the fluff filter on the tumble dryer
● not having lots of posters/papers on walls.

The damage caused by a fire could be reduced by:

● having regular fire drills
● checking equipment on a regular basis
● ensuring all staff/service users know the routine in the event of a fire.

Activity 14

Choose one of the hazards you identified in activities 10 and 11. For this think of how the risk from this hazard may be reduced.

Although you can put plenty of safeguards in place to reduce risks, there is always the chance that they might not be enough. Sometimes events may occur that you cannot plan for. Staff may simply forget, or not follow procedures properly, or an unpredictable event may occur.

4 Examine the main principles of health and safety legislation and guidelines for health and social care environments

There are a number of pieces of legislation that exist to maintain our health and safety. Some of the main ones are listed below with a brief explanation.

Health and Safety at Work Act 1974

This is the main piece of health and safety legislation in the UK. The 1974 Act gives both employers and employees information about their duties to promote health and safety. The law expects employers to look at the risks to health and safety that exist within their workplace and take reasonable measures to reduce the risk of these occurring. For example, the responsibilities of **employers** are to provide a safe place for employees to work in, and to train, inform, instruct and supervise them. The responsibilities of **employees** are to take reasonable care for their own health and safety and to co-operate with and follow health and safety guidelines.

Manual Handling Operations Regulations 1992 (amended 2002)

These regulations cover activities such as lifting, lowering, pushing, pulling or carrying (this includes people). The Health & Safety Executive (HSE) reports that more than a third of injuries that last more than three days are due to poor manual handling (*source*: HSE, 2006). If there is the possibility of injury due to manual handling (such as carrying people or heavy items), then the employer should assess the risk. They should then put measures in place to reduce or avoid the risk. Employees also have responsibilities, such as correctly following procedures and co-operating on all health and safety issues.

Activity 15

Research the correct way to lift items. You could have a look at www.hse.gov.uk and read the advice about frequent or heavy lifting, and using lifting and handling aids.

Food Safety Act 1990

This act states that people working with food must make sure that they practise good food hygiene. If you work with food you must ensure the food is not dangerous to health, and you must also keep good food hygiene within the workplace.

Food Safety (General Food Hygiene Regulations) 1995

This is all about identifying possible risks surrounding food hygiene and putting checks and controls in place to ensure that any risk is reduced.

Reporting of Injuries, Diseases and Dangerous Occurrences Regulations (RIDDOR) 2002

This legislation relates to injuries, diseases and dangerous occurrences. As well as recording these events they must be reported to the Health & Safety Executive. Events that are reportable include death within the workplace, an injury of an employee that results in them being off work for more than three days, and certain illnesses. Dangerous occurrences which happened must also be reported, even if they did not result in injury. A dangerous occurrence could be an electrical short circuit or an explosion of some kind (*source*: HSE).

The Management of Health and Safety at Work Regulations 1999

Under this law, employers have a responsibility to train staff in health and safety. This covers all areas of health and safety legislation such as preventing fire or moving and handling appropriately. It also requires employers to carry out risk assessments.

The Control of Substances Hazardous to Health (COSHH) 2002

This act covers all substances used within the workplace. It covers aspects such as storing, using and disposing of substances. It means that employers should consider the possible risks that these substances present and then take measures to reduce the risk.

Activity 16

Towards P5, M4.

Using the HSE website (www.hse.gov.uk), research the legislation listed above. Try to find out the key information about each law and present this information in a poster or booklet.

SUMMARY

- Individuals have a variety of needs within society – different people will have different needs.

- These include physical, intellectual, emotional and social needs or by looking at a pyramid of needs, such as Maslow's Hierarchy of Needs.

- There are many factors which can impact upon the health and needs of individuals within society.

- Health and social care settings can present a number of potential hazards. Techniques can be put in place to reduce these hazards.

- Health and safety legislation exists which should be followed to reduce the risk of these hazards occurring.

- The Health & Safety Executive is in charge of much of this legislation in the UK and is responsible for ensuring that risks to people's health and safety at work are properly controlled.

- This legislation leads to responsibilities for both employers and employees, in terms of establishing and correctly following the agreed procedures.

Grading grid

In order to pass this unit, the evidence that the learner presents for assessment needs to demonstrate that they can meet all of the learning outcomes for the unit. The criteria for a pass grade describe the level of achievement required to pass this unit.

Grading criteria		
To achieve a pass grade the evidence must show that the learner is able to:	To achieve a merit grade the evidence must show that, in addition to the pass criteria, the learner is able to:	To achieve a distinction grade the evidence must show that, in addition to the pass and merit criteria, the learner is able to:
P1 describe the everyday needs of individuals in society	M1 explain the potential effects of four factors that can influence the health and subsequent needs of individuals in society	D1 explain the potential physical, social and emotional effects on the individual achieving the targets in the action plan
P2 identify the potential effects of four factors that can influence the health and subsequent needs of individuals in society	M2 describe factors which may influence the ability of the individual to adhere to an action plan	D2 explain the strengths and weaknesses of actions taken to minimise risks in health and social care environments
P3 produce a realistic action plan to improve the health of a chosen individual	M3 describe methods to reduce risks in health and social care environments	
P4 identify potential hazards in health and social care environments	M4 explain the main principles of health and safety legislation and guidelines for health and social care environments	
P5 describe the main principles of health and safety legislation and guidelines for health and social care environments		

Vocational Experience in a Health or Social Care Setting

Work experience is strongly recommended for the BTEC First Certificate and Diploma. Working in a real setting helps you realise that health and social care is not just a subject to be studied in textbooks but is real life. When you listen to residents in a care home or help a child in a nursery you are working in the real world.

In this unit you will learn how to:

- apply for a voluntary placement
- prepare and practise for a job interview
- use interpersonal skills in the care setting
- reflect on skills and the knowledge you have gained
- complete a minimum of 60 hours in a health or social care setting.

The unit draws on all the other units and gives you a chance to put into practice the communication skills covered in Unit 1. It also allows you to gather evidence for Unit 7 with creative and therapeutic activities in health and social care. You should be able to use your application letter and interview as evidence for key skills communication. If you word-process your letter it may also provide evidence for ICT key skills. The wider key skills of improving own learning and performance may be covered in your reflective accounts. Working with others may be evidenced by your performance in placement.

Learning Outcomes

On completion of this unit you should be able to:

1 Complete the application process for a period of work experience in a health or social care setting

2 Complete a period of work experience in a health or social care setting

3 Demonstrate the use of interpersonal skills on work experience

4 Describe a period of work experience in a health or social care setting.

1 Complete the application process for a period of work experience in a health or social care setting

This may be the first time you have applied for work experience and it may seem a bit daunting, but it is really quite straightforward if you use common sense.

First of all, put yourself in the position of a care home manager or a nursery manager. They are busy people, short of time, managing in a health and care setting where they must make sure everyone is safe. They may get enquiries every day from people who want to work there or want to place service users there. Reading your application to be a volunteer is not necessarily at the top of their list of priorities. If they get time to look at your letter of application, what do you think would impress them? A scrappy note with spelling mistakes in handwriting they cannot read? Or would they prefer a neatly typed, word-processed, correctly spelled letter which tells them all they need in a concise way? You guessed it – they need to be able to read it easily and quickly!

Personal information/methods

Application procedures vary from job to job, but most applications require you to provide some information about yourself: what you want to do, why you want to do the job and how you think you are suited for the job.

Good questions to keep in mind are:

- who
- what
- why
- how
- when
- where.

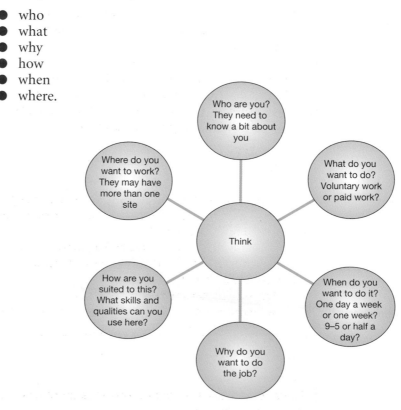

Think about your job application

Activity 1

Make a mind map like the one on page 54 and answer the questions about yourself and the work you want to do. This will help you with the next activities.

Did you know?

Curriculum vitae comes from Latin. 'Curriculum' means the course, as in 'the course of a stream'. 'Vitae' means life. So 'curriculum vitae' means 'the course of one's life'.

CV stands for curriculum vitae. It is a brief summary of your life and is an important document to get right. Employers often make snap judgements about you based on your CV.

- You have five seconds to make an impression.
- Your CV may go in the bin if it is not clear.
- Your CV may go in the bin if it is too complicated or fancy.
- Your CV may go in the bin if there are spelling mistakes.
- Your CV may go in the bin if it is scruffy, has smudges or stains or smells of nicotine.

So, how can we save yours from going in the bin?

The key to a good CV

- Try to keep to one page, but if it looks cramped, go on to a second page.
- Make the information easy to find. Remember, managers are busy people.
- Be truthful.
- Use best-quality A4-sized paper.
- Do not attach certificates – take them to the interview.
- Attach a covering letter saying how you meet the requirements for this job.
- When you have finished your CV, read it and re-read it, then ask another person to read it to spot any mistakes.

Include the following sections:
1. Name, address and contact details.
2. Skills.
3. Experience – you may not have much at this point but perhaps you have done babysitting or helped an elderly neighbour with their garden.
4. Immediate career goals.
5. Career history – have you had a part-time job?
6. Education – what did you achieve at school?
7. Interests and hobbies.
8. Any other relevant personal details.
9. References – if you are in education your teacher should be the first referee.

Remember

Never criticise a school or a previous employer – you may need their help for future references.

Activity 2

Towards P1.
Draft your CV and have it checked by your tutor.

Application forms are sometimes used. If you are asked to complete an application form, make sure you fill in every box required. Leaving gaps gives the impression you cannot follow basic instructions, or, even worse, that you don't care. It is a good idea to photocopy the form first and work on the practice copy. Then you can change it if you make any mistakes. Once you have the right information in the right box, transferring it to the best copy is easy.

If you are asked to send a **letter of application,** include the basic information you would have put in a CV but make sure it is tailored for the job you are applying for. You may like making cakes as a hobby but it is not really relevant if you are applying for a job as a paramedic. Your clean driving licence is much more relevant to the job.

Activity 3

Which of these might you include in a letter of application for a job or placement at nursery?

- Your best friend's name.
- Your name.
- Your previous experience helping your aunt with twins.
- Your previous disasters with cooking.
- Your ability to use British Sign Language.
- The fact that you have a current first aid certificate.

Discuss this with a partner and compare your ideas.

Did you know?

The BBC website has lots of tips on letter writing. Check it out at www.bbc.co.uk/skillswise.

Letters to accept/decline

Some employers may ask you to write to confirm you accept or decline the job. It is good manners to do this as soon as possible. If they have offered you a job and you want to accept it, you need to let them know as soon as possible. If you do not want it, you need to let them know so they can offer it to someone else. In either case, do remember to thank them for offering you the job.

Appropriate content and format

Here are two letters – which do you think would be better if applying for a volunteer placement?

Letter 1

Hiya there
Wndrn if u have a job 4 me?
I'm gr8 with old folks and can shout really loud.
I wnt to wrk Mon & Tues 10–3 as I have to pck up kids frm schl.
Txt bck if ok. 0789XXX
Lv
Sal

Letter 2

12 Rose Terrace
Onetown
OX1 XXX

Telephone 0789XXX

12 October 20XX

Dear Mrs Siddons

I am writing to ask if you would accept me as a volunteer at Sunnyside care home.

I am 16 years old, a student on a health and social care course and I have a clear CRB police check.

I helped my grandmother after she had a stroke and found I really enjoyed helping her to speak again. I am hoping to develop my career working with older people and eventually I would like to apply for nursing.

I am able to attend placement on Monday or Tuesday from 9am to 4pm from the beginning of December through until the end of March. I have permission from my college to attend if you decide to offer me an interview.

I hope to hear from you soon.

Yours sincerely

Sally Jones

The first letter is informal and very casual. The format is fine between friends or in a text message, but is not suitable to impress an employer. The second letter is formal and says who the person is and what they want as well as what they can offer the residents. The second person has taken time to think about the letter and spell words correctly. She has highlighted her previous experience and what she can offer. The first person seems more interested in her own needs.

Writing a letter takes practice. Make a list of everything you want to include. Look at the advice for CVs if you are not sure. Write all your ideas on Post-Its first, then put them into order. Draft your letter and check for spelling and grammar. Then ask a teacher or someone else to read it. Listen to their suggestions and re-draft your letter. You may need two or three drafts before it is right.

Use of ICT

Most people use ICT to write letters. Here are some advantages and disadvantages of using ICT and handwriting. Can you add more ideas in each box?

	ICT	Handwriting
Advantages	Spell-check Grammar-check Move items around easily Make changes easily Looks professional You can keep a copy easily	Personal
Disadvantages	Can seem impersonal Poor layout may spoil the effect	Mistakes in spelling, grammar and layout give a poor impression

Activity 4

Towards P1.
Write a letter to apply for a place as a volunteer at a health and social care setting of your choice.

Interview skills

Sam wants a voluntary placement at Sunnyside residential home. She has applied and been given a date and time for interview. What advice could you give her about:

- punctuality?
- social and personal skills?
- communication skills?
- relating to others – body language?
- listening?
- answering questions?
- asking questions?

Punctuality

Punctuality means being on time. It is very important to be on time for an interview because it shows you are interested in the job and that you are reliable. Make sure you know where the interview is and how to get there at that time of day. If you are travelling by bus, do the buses run at that time? How long does it take to get there? Have you allowed for any roadworks or traffic problems? If you are punctual you will feel more relaxed for the interview.

Social and personal skills

People may make judgements about you based on your social skills. See the following case study.

Case Study

Sam was running late for her interview and had only five minutes to spare. She arrived at reception and asked the way to the interview room. The receptionist told her to take the first door on the right and follow the corridor to the end. As Sam got to the door, a resident approached, walking slowly using a walking frame. Sam knew she did not have much time to spare and for a split second thought of rushing through and letting the door slam on the resident, but she could not do it. She held the door open even though it cost her precious minutes. As she hurried down the corridor she worried she might be late.

The interview was delayed for a short while because one of the panel members was late. Imagine Sam's surprise when the panel member arrived and it was the same person she had held the door for earlier! Sam got the job because they were impressed with her good manners.

Social skills matter, especially when you work with people. If you leave rubbish behind when you have a snack, people may think you are lazy and untidy. If you speak rudely, they may think you do not know how to interact with others. If you are quarrelsome and argumentative, they may not want to work with you. If you swear, even if it is just with your friends, people may judge that you do not know how to behave.

Communication skills

Activity 5

Look back at Unit 1 to remind yourself about communication skills.

In communication, 55 per cent is down to body language; 38 per cent is the tone of voice; only 7 per cent relates to the words we say (Mehrabian, 1971).

Relating to others

How you relate to others shows in your body language. If you are anxious, your face may be tense and unwelcoming. This can appear to others as anger or disapproval. You may be nervous but they might think you are not interested. If you chew your nails they will know you are scared.

Lack of eye contact gives the impression you do not want to be there. You may just be nervous or you may be from a culture where it is rude to make eye contact. Make an effort to look up and make eye contact with the people around you, so you appear confident even if you do not feel it.

Tense, anxious body language

Looking away and hesitating when speaking makes you seem unsure of yourself. Physical barriers show someone is feeling threatened. Crossed arms, crossed legs or holding an object in front of you all form protective barriers and show you feel defensive. Try to keep your body language open. Turn to the person you are talking to, keep your arms and legs uncrossed. Your hands should be open and relaxed. This way you will seem confident even if inside you are nervous.

How to give the message you DON'T care

If you really want to get rid of someone, fidgeting and tapping your foot shows you are bored and makes them feel unwelcome. Looking over their shoulder and looking round the room when they are talking to you gives the message you have not got time for them.

If you really want to put people off you, listen to music through your headphones.

Do not try any of these things during an interview!

How to give the impression you DO care

Stand up straight.

Make eye contact.

Smile and look around.

Keep your arms relaxed at your sides.

Keep both feet on the floor.

Look at each person on the interview panel while speaking. This shows you respect them equally.

The best place to make eye contact with another person is the area from the nose to the eyes.

Your body language can give you away. Communication experts can usually tell when people are not telling the truth.

Activity 6

Try this with a partner. Think of one thing that is true and interests you and one thing which is not true. Talk to your partner for one minute about each.
Do they notice any change in your body language when you change from a true to an untrue subject?
Do it in a different order so they do not know which the true situation is and which the untrue situation is.
Can they tell which the true situation is and when you are not telling the truth?

Source: www.CartoonStock.com

What changed? Did you look away when telling a lie? Or touch your ear or nose? Perhaps your hand went to your mouth? These are indicators when we are not sure or are uncomfortable with what we are doing or saying.

Listening

Listening is an important part of interview skills. Sometimes when people are nervous they do not hear what is said. If you are nervous, take some slow, deep breaths. If you have not understood, you can ask the interviewer to repeat the question.

Answering questions and asking questions

Do not feel you have to rush. Take a little time to think about the question you are asked. Experienced interviewers know to ask one question at a time, but not every interviewer is experienced. If they ask you more than one question at once, try to answer each part carefully.

At the end of an interview *you* are often invited to ask questions. It is always a good idea to prepare one or two questions. This shows you have thought about the organisation and really are interested. It is not usually the best time to ask about salary if you are applying for a paid job. Wait until you are offered the job before discussing pay.

Preparation for interview

Telephone skills

The first impression the organisation has of you may well be when you speak to them on the telephone. It is a good idea to develop a standard way of answering the telephone so that it is an automatic response. A polite and friendly tone is more important than what you say. Most people use a polite 'Hello' when answering a call. If it is an official ringing, you can then increase the formality of your responses. If it is your friend, you can become less formal. Unfortunately it is difficult to correct a poor first impression. If you answer the telephone using a curt, angry tone, they may think you are unapproachable – perhaps not the best way to impress an employer.

If you telephone an organisation, prepare what you want to say. Do not assume they have all the time in the world to listen to you. If you telephone and speak to a receptionist, always be polite. Explain who you need to speak to and why. You do not need to go into detail but the receptionist may be able to re-direct your call if the person you need is away. When you are put through to the person you need to speak to, be brief. Say who you are and why you are telephoning. At that point they may be able to help you or tell you who is a better person to answer your questions.

If you are telephoning about a job advertisement, say what job it is and where you saw the advertisement. They may then take your details and send you an application form along with a list of what they are looking for. Often these are listed as essential criteria – what you must have – and then desirable criteria – what it would be nice to have. There may be a person specification as well as a job specification. Read them carefully to see whether the job is what you thought it was. At this point you may decide to apply. Use the method they ask for. If they send you an application form, complete it. If they ask for three copies of your CV, send three copies. If they ask for a letter of application, send one.

When you telephone it is not an opportunity to tell them your life story or ask for careers advice. They may be in the middle of an important job when you ring.

Activity 7

Role-play a situation where you ring an organisation to ask for details about a job. One person should answer the telephone, one person should make the phone call and one person should observe.
The observer should make a list of what went well and what should be improved.

Knowledge of interview procedures

Knowing what to expect reduces your anxiety levels.

Arrive at the right place at the right time and tell them you are here. You will probably be asked to sit down and may be offered a cup of coffee or tea. It is probably better to thank them but decline the offer of a drink. If you are really nervous, the last thing you want is to be juggling a cup and saucer. A glass of water is a better option if your lips are dry.

You may be waiting with others applying for the same post. If you are, be friendly and smile.

When you are called into the interview room, walk tall and smile, making eye contact with everyone. Formal interviews usually consist of a panel of three interviewers. This is so that when they discuss the candidates later, they do not have an even split of votes but have to decide 2 to 1. One person generally takes the lead and explains what will happen. The usual procedure is for one person to ask questions which you answer, then the next interviewer asks their questions which you answer and so on. At the end you are usually invited to ask your questions. Interviewers often make notes about how you meet (or do not meet) the criteria for the job.

In a formal interview situation it is not usual to be told there and then whether you have the post – they often telephone you or write to you. If you are applying for a voluntary position you may sometimes be told if you have got it at that point. Never assume they have to have you. They are doing you a favour if they let you do voluntary work with their service users in their organisation.

Always thank them for their time. If you get the post they know they have someone with good manners. If you do not get the post, thank them for their time and ask for feedback so that you know what to improve on next time you have an interview.

Role play

Try this in class. Get a job advertisement from the local press or a health and social care journal. You can also get one from the NHS jobs website (http://www.jobs.nhs.uk/). Here is a job description from the NHS website (reproduced under the terms of the Click–Use licence). It has been shortened but it is still quite long.

JOB DESCRIPTION
POST: Bank Healthcare Assistant
RESPONSIBLE TO: Ward Sister
ACCOUNTABLE TO: Clinical Workforce Manager

JOB SUMMARY

- To work as part of a team to provide a welcoming, caring, friendly and safe environment for patients and their families.
- To carry out assigned tasks as directed, under the supervision of the qualified nursing staff.
- To be proactive in monitoring and anticipating patients' needs within the boundaries of the job description and communicate effectively with the multidisciplinary team.

Continued overleaf

Person specification for Healthcare assistant on the Nurse Bank

REQUIREMENTS	CRITERIA	ESSENTIAL/ DESIRABLE	HOW ASSESSED?* A = Application form I = Interview
1 Education/ Qualifications/ Training	● Good standard of education including literacy and numeracy	E	A
	● NVQ level 2 in care or equivalent experience	D	A
	● GCSE English or equivalent	D	A
	● Basic food hygiene		
	Mandatory training:		
	● Basic life support	E	A
	● Infection control	E	A
	● Moving and handling	E	A
	● Fire	E	A
2 Skills/Abilities	● Good communication skills, both written and verbal, at all levels within a multidisciplinary team	E	I
	● Good organisational skills	E	I
	● Able to work as part of a team	E	I
	● Ability to work independently and under supervision	E	I
	● Basic computer skills	D	A
3 Experience	● At least 12 months' experience in a hospital setting	E	I
	● Able to take and record patient observations – temperature, pulse, respirations, urinalysis	D	I
	● Previous experience in child-healthcare setting	E	I
	● Experience of dealing with the public	E	I

Continued overleaf

REQUIREMENTS	CRITERIA	ESSENTIAL/ DESIRABLE	HOW ASSESSED?* A = Application form I = Interview
4 Knowledge	● Knowledge and understanding of the health service	E	I
	● Providing a safe environment for children	E	I
	● Knowledge and understanding of the needs of children and families	E	I
	● Awareness of cultural and spiritual needs	D	I
5 Other requirements	● Enthusiastic and motivated	E	I
	● Caring and approachable	E	I
	● Good interpersonal skills	E	I
	● Professional approach to work	E	I
	● Accountability – takes responsibility for own actions and promotes good team working	E	I
	● Openness – shares information and good practice appropriately	E	I
	● Mutual respect – treats others with courtesy and respect at all times	E	I

Activity 8

Note down all those requirements which will be assessed at interview (they have 'I' next to them). Make a set of questions to assess these attributes. For example, to assess 'Good communication skills, both written and verbal, at all levels within a multidisciplinary team', you may have a question such as 'Tell me when you have used written communication skills in the care setting'. You will, of course, be able to assess their verbal communication skills by the way they explain their answer. Make sure you have a question to check everything that needs to be assessed at interview.

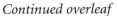

Continued overleaf

Activity 8 (continued)

Then have four volunteers to do the role play. Decide who is going to be interviewed and who is on the interview panel. Set the room as an interview room, with three chairs at one side of the table for the interviewers and one chair at the other side of the table for the person being interviewed.
Each member of the interview panel prepares two questions, which they discuss with the other panel members.

The person being interviewed will need to wait outside until they are called into the room. The interviewers will need to explain what will happen to the person being interviewed when they bring them in and they will need to conduct the interview appropriately.

The rest of the class form the audience and complete feedback sheets, commenting on the effectiveness of the communication skills of every member of the panel as well as the candidate.
A schedule such as the one below may help.

	First Impressions	Body language	Eye contact	Verbal responses	Other comments
Interviewer 1					
Interviewer 2					
Interviewer 3					
Candidate					

If the feedback is honest it will be valuable for those observed.

Activity 9

After the first role play, split into smaller groups and get a different job advertisement and repeat the process. Try to make sure everyone has a turn at being interviewed and getting some feedback from an observer.

Transport planning

Use a reliable means of transport for getting to your interview!

Make sure you know the bus routes and the bus timetable if you are travelling by bus. If you are driving, where will you park? You may need to check that they have a car park and that you are allowed to use it. Find out how far the car park is from where your interview is to take place. You do not want to get lost on the way from the car park. Allow plenty of time. The unexpected does happen. There may be roadworks or a road traffic accident, or you may get a puncture, or the bus may break down. Plan to arrive 20 minutes early so you have time to spare.

Dress code

Always look clean and tidy. Even if the dress code is casual it does not mean scruffy. Clean your shoes. This is not the time for exposing cleavage or hairy chests! Avoid too much jewellery or make-up. Your appearance should convey the message that you are sensible and reliable, not that you are out for a good time. Make sure you make a good first impression and half the battle is over. First impressions do count.

Attitude

Your attitude shows in your body language, in how you say things and also in what you say. A person who chews gum during an interview is either unaware that it is rude or does not care. In either case they are unlikely to get the job. Employers often classify people into two types – the 'Can do's' and the 'Can't do's'. Which type of person would you rather work with?

A person with a 'can do' attitude says	A person with a 'can't do' attitude says
'I'll have a go. . .'	'I'm not doing that. . .'
'I'll try my best. . .'	'No way. . .'
'I'm not sure if it will work but let's try it. . .'	'You must be joking if you think I'm doing that.'
'I've always done it that way but I'm willing to try something different.'	'I'm not going to try it.'
	'I've always done it that way and I'm not changing.'

Prioritising

Interview skills and life skills call for us to get our priorities in order. Which matters more to you – going out with your mates the night before an interview and risking oversleeping or being fresh for the interview and getting the job?

List of questions

Always find out as much as you can about the organisation before the interview.

Activity 10

Choose an organisation where you would like to volunteer.
Make a list of questions and try to find out the answers yourself.
These are some where **you** *can find the answers*.
What type of work do they do?
What service user groups do they care for?
Is it daycare or residential?
Is it a voluntary organisation or a private one or part of the state system?
What was the last inspection report like? (You can see all inspection reports on the Commission for Social Care Inspection website at http://www.csci.org.uk.)
What do they do well?
What do they need to improve on?

Questions you may wish to ask at interview

What training do they give to new staff?

What opportunities are there to develop your career with the organisation?

What changes do they think may happen to the organisation in the future?

How do they plan to build on their strengths (if the latest inspection report was good)?

Activity 11

Towards P2.
Role-play an interview situation. If possible, bring in a manager from a local care home to be part of the interview panel. They may also be able to bring along some of their staff to make up the rest of the panel to make it more realistic.
Use appropriate interview skills for a health or social care work experience placement.
Written feedback from the interview panel may provide evidence for you as a witness testimony sheet.

These questions show you want to be involved and are willing to learn new skills to add to those you already have. The last question shows you are interested in the organisation, have already read the report and know what they do well.

2 Complete a period of work experience in a health or social care setting

Remember – when you do work experience you are representing your school or college. If you make a good impression they will be willing to offer more learners the chance to volunteer with them. Your school or college will make sure that all placements have been checked for safety and suitability.

You will need to have a Criminal Records Bureau (CRB) check. Some placements also require a Protection of Vulnerable Adults (POVA) check before you can volunteer there.

Organisation

Health and social care is provided in three ways:

● statutory
● voluntary
● private.

Statutory provision is provided by the state (another name for the government) – think 'stat' is in both words.

Statutory provision is paid for by taxes so you do not need to pay at the hospital or when you visit your doctor. In health, state hospitals, clinics, local doctors are part of state provision. In statutory social care we have local authority social services departments which employ social workers to assess the needs of older people, or people with mental health problems, or younger people who need social care.

Voluntary provision is provided by charities. It is paid for by donations from ordinary people. When you see people with collecting tins outside shops they are trying to raise funds for charities. People who use voluntary services sometimes make a small donation for the help they get, but often it is help which is given for free.

Private provision in health and social care is funded by charging fees. Some people use private health care because they can have it when they want it rather than having to wait. A health check may cost £430–£460 for an hour (see the BUPA website at http://www.bupa.co.uk/wellness/asp/personal/health_assessments/best_choice/index.asp#). A two-hour session will include 45 minutes with a doctor. Tests may include some blood tests for thyroid function or tests for prostate cancer for men.

Private social care charges fees to residents. Many older people in residential homes pay over £400 per week to stay there. Some care home fees are over £800 per week (see the CSCI website at http://www.csci.org.uk).

Activity 12

Find out what local provision there is in your area for health care and then find out what there is for social care.

Write the names on Post-Its and try to fit them onto a grid like the one below.

Health care – state	Health care – voluntary	Health care – private
Social care – state	Social care – voluntary	Social care – private

As you work through this, try to decide whether they are statutory, voluntary or private providers.

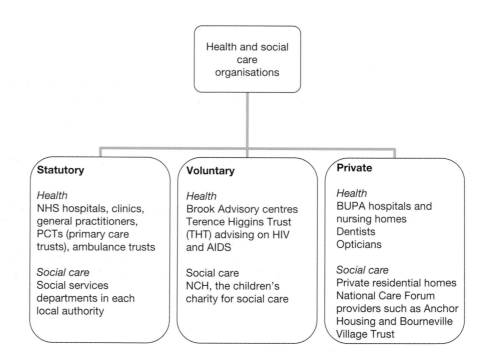

Choice of organisation/placement appropriate to the learner

Finding what is available in your area may help you to decide where you want to have your placement. Some people choose a placement because they already have some experience of working with people in health care or social care. Some people choose a placement because they have never worked in that area and want to know what it is like. It is a good idea to try something new. If you then decide to make your career in health and social care you will have broader experience on which to base your career choices.

Activity 13

Towards P3.
Complete a period of work experience in a health or social care setting. You need to attend for at least 60 hours. Make sure you get your log book signed very time you attend. Don't leave it until the end of your placement or the person you need may be on holiday!

3 Demonstrate the use of interpersonal skills on work experience

Activity 14

Look back at Unit 1 and make sure you have practised your interpersonal skills before you go into placement.

Skills you may need to think about once you are in placement are as follows.

Overcoming communication barriers

In your placement you will meet people with different communication needs. Some people need a brightly lit room if they are lip-reading. Others can hear a little if the television is turned down. Sometimes you need to adapt your voice so they can hear.

Case Study

Nargus has a placement at Springfield Nursing Home. At lunchtime when she helps Mrs Brown to cut up her food, she makes sure she sits facing her so that Mrs Brown can read her lips.

Tact and diplomacy

Here is an example of when you need tact and diplomacy. Diplomacy means being skilful, subtle and discreet.

Activity 15

Sometimes it is very busy in the nursing home. Nargus is concerned because sometimes patients ring their buzzers and do not get attention for several minutes. Of course she goes to answer the buzzers when she is free but she is not allowed to take people to the toilet. When she answers a buzzer and someone wants the toilet, she tells the senior care assistant, Marian, who says 'I'll be there as soon as I can.' Sometimes it is too late and the patient has wet the bed.

What would you do? Discuss this with a partner and see how many solutions you can come up with.

See Activity 15. Here are some possible things Nargus could do:

1 She could report Marian to the senior nurse in charge for not answering the buzzer.
2 She could offer to help Marian so that Marian could finish the current job quicker and take the next patient to the toilet.
3 She could find someone else who may be free and tell them about the patient needing to go to the toilet.
4 She could make sure that there are no obstacles in the way and get the patient's slippers and dressing gown ready so that when Marian gets to the patient she does not have to spend time moving things out of the way or searching for slippers.

Which of these show tact and diplomacy? Did you think 2, 3, and 4? Yes, you are right. This shows an understanding of care work and a willingness to help the patient. The first response is not tactful and not diplomatic. It is confrontational. It shows little understanding of the pressures in care work and does nothing to help the patient. It is more about blaming than helping.

Discretion and confidentiality

Discretion means carefulness and good judgment. Sometimes a care worker has information which is confidential. If they are discreet they do not break confidentiality.

Case Study

Marian has been told by the nurse in charge that Mrs Brown has an infection and needs to have her temperature taken every four hours. A visitor asks why she is taking the temperature so often. Marian is discreet and does not tell the visitor about the infection. Instead she says that temperatures are routinely taken for everyone. This maintains confidentiality. The visitor may be a stranger to Mrs Brown. Certainly they have no right to information about her. Marian is friendly and polite but does not tell other people about her patient. She knows who has a right to know, and does not gossip about her patients.

Ability to follow instructions

Being able to follow instructions is an important skill in care work. Sometimes a life may depend on it.

Case Study

Sally has a placement at the local hospital. She is on the rehabilitation ward and enjoys working with patients to get them mobile again. Most people are recovering slowly but surely. One day she is talking to a patient when she hears a crash. She turns round to see Mr Green on the floor. His walking frame has fallen too. He is very pale and his lips are blue. The nurse in charge hurries over and checks his airway, breathing and pulse, then starts CPR. She calls for the senior care to ring for help, then asks Sally to bring the emergency trolley and draw the screens. Sally does this, then the senior care comes back and asks her to move the other patients to the day room at the other end of the ward as some of them are getting upset.

Because Sally follows instructions, the care Mr Green gets is the best in the situation. She brings the emergency trolley so the nurse can get any equipment she needs. This frees the senior care assistant to telephone for help. Sally moves the other patients away so the nurse and senior care can focus on Mr Green. If she had said no, or had not been listening, his care would have been delayed. Sally showed the ability to follow instructions and also that she was a good team worker.

Activity 16

Towards P4.
Look back at the communication cycle in Unit 1 and think how it can be applied in your placement. Ask your placement supervisor to observe you in a one-to-one interaction and then in a group interaction and to give you some written feedback
Describe your strengths and weaknesses in interpersonal skills at work placement.

4 Describe a period of work experience in a health or social care setting

Organisation

The organisation where you do your voluntary placement may be part of the statutory, voluntary or private sector. As we saw earlier they are each funded differently. The private sector charges the full cost and a little more to make a profit. Voluntary organisations try to keep the services free or at very little cost to the person who needs them. The state or statutory sector gets money from taxes so that some basic care is 'free at point of delivery'. People pay taxes so they do not have to pay when they are ill. Look back to Unit 1 for more detail about the welfare state and the NHS.

Did you know?

Before we had the National Health Service, if you needed to see the doctor you had to pay. Poor people could not afford to pay and so did not always get the health care they needed. Many people died because they were ill and poor.

Funding

Funding, or paying for care, is a topic that many people feel strongly about. Read these two case studies and see what you think.

Case Studies

Mr S worked hard all his life and saved. He was very proud when he bought his council house. It was their own home. Although it was difficult to keep up the mortgage repayments, they managed. His two children were always well dressed but they could not have the most expensive trainers. They got teased at school because they could not keep up with fashion. They were the last to get mobile phones and even then they were the basic models. Just before the children left school, the family had their first holiday abroad – a week self-catering in Spain.

Just before Mr S was due to retire he had a stroke. After a while in hospital he was discharged home. He was not expected to speak again and needed help to shower. A social worker came to assess his needs and to do a financial assessment. He had saved all his life and had £30,000 in the bank, so he could not get any help with his care needs. He had to pay carers £11 per hour to help him. Only when his savings dropped to £13,500 could he get free care.

Mr V next door had had a job once on a farm, picking fruit and sorting potatoes, but it didn't last. He got fired for not turning up on time. He was glad in a way because he could spend more time down the pub with his mates. He had six kids and got enough money with what he made on the side and the benefits. They went on holiday twice a year and the kids always got what they wanted. He didn't believe in saving. When he was 60 he had a heart attack and needed care at home. He had no savings so he got all the care he needed free. Social services paid for it because he had no savings.

Activity 17

Discuss these case studies with your class, then suggest how the system could be made fairer.

Resources needed and resources available

Resources include money, time, people and equipment. There is always a gap between what resources are needed and what are available.

Resources needed	Resources available
Money to pay for more staff	Limited amount of money from taxes
More time to spend with patients in clinics	Timed appointments so everyone gets seen
More nurses to care for people	Limited number of funded training places
More operating theatres to get waiting lists down	Limited number of staff so cannot staff any more theatres

The only ways to get more resources for health and social care are to either increase taxes or spend less on education, transport and defence.

Policies and procedures

Policies are plans or general guidelines. Procedures spell out how to do something.

- There may be a health and safety **policy** giving general guidelines.
- But there is a **procedure** for disposing of sharp needles.

Here are some examples.

Activity 18

Find out what **policies** there are at your work placement and what **procedures** you are expected to follow.

Policies	Procedures
Equality and diversity	Complaints procedure
Health and safety	Safe disposal of sharps
Data protection	Recording and reporting
Staff recruitment and Training	Checking staff against the POVA list

Health and safety

Health and safety is everyone's responsibility all the time. You can never switch off.

Case Study

Tania, a staff nurse, works at the local hospital on a busy orthopaedic ward. They are very keen on health and safety and everyone has been trained in manual handling. They use the hoists and the correct sling when moving people.

One evening at about 8.30 p.m. Tania is about to go off duty when Mr X in the end bed needs an injection. She checks the prescription chart and sees he can have his next injection. She checks the drug with another nurse and draws up the drug correctly, placing the needle and syringe in a tray. She takes the yellow sharps box with her to the bedside, checks Mr X's name and number and gives the injection, then turns to dispose of the sharp needle. As she pushes the needle into the box, she feels a sharp prick. The box was nearly full and a needle was not in the box properly.

Fig 3.5

A sharps bin

Tania had to go to casualty at once and have a blood test. Mr X was asked to consent to a blood test for HIV. Luckily for Tania it came back clear, otherwise her career could have been at an end and her health threatened.

Tania followed a lot of procedures correctly but made one mistake. She should have closed the bin that was nearly full and got a new bin. Many accidents happen when people are tired or busy. It takes only one mistake to cause an accident.

Activity 19

In pairs, discuss the following. What health and safety issues are there at your placement? What is done about them? What do you do about them?

Multicultural factors

Multi means many. Culture is to do with our customs and habits, the way we live. Multicultural means many ways to live. In our multicultural society we have many ways of celebrating. Some people throw a party. Some people get so drunk they are physically sick. Some people celebrate with music or fireworks or both. In some cultures the birth of a new baby is celebrated joyfully. In other cultures they may celebrate only if it is a boy.

Different cultures deal differently with illness. In some cultures mental illness carries a stigma and people feel ashamed that anyone in their family has a mental illness. They may deny it or try to hide it from friends and neighbours. In some cultures death is seen as a tragedy, something to be very sad about. In cultures where people have a strong religious faith, they may not view death as a sad event but rather as passing to a better place. In your placement you will meet people with cultures which are different to yours. Try to find out about their cultures and share yours. Try to keep an open mind and do not judge people who are different from you.

Activity 20

Start a multicultural notebook. Make a list of all the different cultures represented in your placement. Don't forget to include staff and regular visitors. There may be different religions or languages. Find out one thing you did not previously know about that culture or religion. Learn how to say 'Hello' in a different language. Each time you learn something new, add it to your notebook.

Staff

Staffing levels

Staff wages are one of the biggest expenses in any health and care budget. Public provision is funded by the government so NHS staff wages are one of the biggest expenses on the taxpayer. The Audit Commission tries to make sure that the government gets best value for money. A 2001 survey of acute hospitals by the Audit Commission found that teaching hospitals spent more on staffing but could not show a better improvement in patient care than those which spent less money on staffing.

Did you know?

Trusts cannot demonstrate a link between the amount spent on ward staffing and the quality of care they deliver.
Source: Audit Commission's Acute Hospital Portfolio (November 2001, no. 3).

One thing is certain – wherever you work you will find that much of the basic care work is done by care assistants rather than professionally qualified nurses. Student nurses are supernumerary, not part of the workforce, and their work is now mostly done by healthcare assistants and clinical support workers. Specialist nurses include community liaison nurses, tissue viability nurses and pain specialists. They may visit the ward to see a patient but do not work on that ward. There are more patients but fewer registered nurses.

A 2005 survey by the Royal College of Nursing found there were staffing ratios of 7.7 patients per registered nurse during the day and 10.1 per registered nurse during the night. In the private sector this was 5.5 during the day. See graph overleaf.

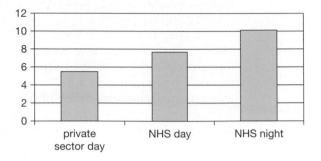

Staffing ratios (number of patients per registered nurse)

The 2005 Healthcare Commission report, 'Ward Staffing', found that staffing levels were based not on patients' needs but on tradition. They also found a higher level of complaints when there was a higher level of temporary or 'bank' staff (*source*: http://www.healthcarecommission.org.uk/serviceproviderinformation/reviewsand studies/servicereviews/ahpmethodology/wardstaffing.cfm). In social care the situation is much the same. There are fewer qualified people and many more unqualified staff having to take on work those professionals once did.

Activity 21

Have a class debate. One side takes the view 'We need more trained nurses'. The other side takes the view 'We need more care assistants'. List your reasons, debate for 15 minutes, then vote.

Professional qualifications in health and social care can be achieved in a number of ways: through becoming a qualified nurse with either a three-year diploma or degree at university, or becoming a qualified social worker following a three-year degree at university. These are the main qualifications to progress up a career ladder. Of course, there are many other professions allied to medicine and health care, such as occupational therapy, speech and language therapy, physiotherapy. These too require a three- or four-year degree in order to qualify. There are also opportunities for occupational therapy assistants, speech and language therapy assistants and physiotherapy assistants.

Did you know?

The NHS has a careers website – http://www.nhscareers.nhs.uk/ – where you can find out about careers and pay in the NHS.

Many people working in care now study for a National Vocational Qualification in health and social care to qualify as a health or social care assistant and study while they work. They need to be hardworking and enthusiastic as well as patient and caring.

Cadet schemes are available in some trusts. They may be up to two years long, include an induction then a variety of work experience in settings such as pharmacy, on the wards, in various departments. Sometimes the schemes include training such as NVQ. This is a good way to see what careers are on offer in the NHS before applying to university for a degree course.

Terms and conditions

These vary in the different sectors. Whether you are qualified or unqualified, if you work in the voluntary sector, your job might depend on funding. If the funding is not available, the job may not continue. The private sector may have a different career structure and pay scale to the statutory sector. In the statutory sector you may find that your contract is flexible, allowing you to work long shifts such as 12 hours for three times per week. The NHS is introducing a skills escalator to provide a career route for staff to develop with a trust rather than move away to other trusts. Unions such as the Royal College of Nursing and Unison negotiate pay deals with the main employers to maintain pay levels.

Ways of monitoring performance

Appraisals are one way to monitor performance. An appraisal is a way of assessing someone or something. It is good practice for employers to appraise staff annually. An appraisal is usually conducted by the person's line manager.

Appraisals vary from a simple tick sheet to a detailed assessment against objectives such as timekeeping, record keeping or reliability. The person being appraised should have a chance to express their views.

Here is an example of appraisal paperwork.

Woodfields care home – appraisal sheet for person being appraised

Please complete and bring this to the appraisal with you.

What I have done well this year...

....

....

What I would like to improve on..

....

....

How I would like to develop my career..

....

....

Appraisal paper worksheet two – to be used at the appraisal interview

Name

Post held

Staff number

Date

Review of last appraisal

Actions met

Actions carried forward

	Excellent	Good	Satisfactory	Not at required standard
Punctuality				
Attendance				
Attitude to work				

Training needs identified yes/no

● health and safety training

● protection of vulnerable adults training

● first aid course

● other

Actions from this appraisal

Comments of appraiser

Signature

Date

Comments of appraisee

Signature

Date

Need/opportunities for continuing professional development

Everyone needs to continue learning. Professionals must keep a record of their professional development. Nurses and midwives may be asked for their professional development record at any time.

The Nursing & Midwifery Council code of professional conduct states that as a registered nurse, midwife or specialist community public health nurse, you are personally accountable for your practice. In caring for patients and service users, you must:

- respect the patient or service user as an individual
- obtain consent before you give any treatment or care
- protect confidential information
- co-operate with others in the team
- maintain your professional knowledge and competence
- be trustworthy
- act to identify and minimise risk to patients and service users.

These are the shared values of all the United Kingdom healthcare regulatory bodies (*source*: http://www.nmc-uk.org).

The General Social Care Council regulates social workers and those who work in social care. They too have a code of conduct. You can find out about it on the Council's website at http://www.gscc.org.uk.

Own performance

Reflecting on your own performance is not easy. If you have done well, it feels good and you are proud to think about what you did well. What about the things that you don't find easy to do? It is harder to think about things we are not good at, but that is how we really learn. If you are honest with yourself, you are your best critic and you are the best person to put things right.

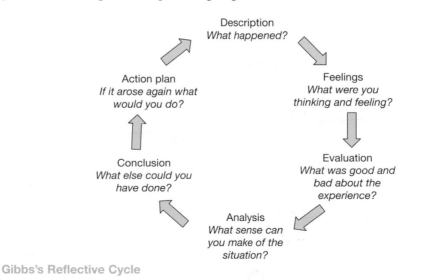

Gibbs's Reflective Cycle

It is important to be honest when you reflect on your practice. There are many ways to reflect on your performance. One way is to use a reflective model such as Gibbs's Reflective Cycle.

1 **Description**
  ● What happened?
  ● How did it happen?
  ● Who was there?
  ● What did you do?
  ● What did they do?
  ● When did it happen?
  ● Why did it happen?
  ● Where did it happen?
2 How did you feel?
3 What was good about the experience? What was not so good?
4 Analysis – break it down into parts. What parts worked and what parts did not?
5 What else could you have done in that situation?
6 If it happened again, what would you do differently?

Another way to reflect is to use the conscious competence model. It has four stages, as shown below.

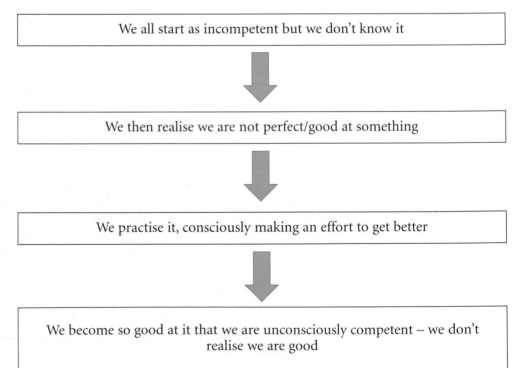

We all start as incompetent but we don't know it

We then realise we are not perfect/good at something

We practise it, consciously making an effort to get better

We become so good at it that we are unconsciously competent – we don't realise we are good

Try it out. Identify one thing you need to improve. Perhaps you are shy and don't know what to do at placement, so you sit in a corner and don't mix with others (unconscious incompetence).

The senior care assistant tells you to stop sitting alone and try talking to residents. You try but find it hard to start a conversation (conscious incompetence). Warning: many people stick at this point and give up (but they may not make good carers). You try again next time and ask Mrs Green about her knitting. She tells you all about her great-granddaughter and the cardigan she is making for her. You realise you can talk to older people and practise starting up conversations with them (conscious competence). Within a few weeks you forget you ever had a problem talking to people and you can chat easily to anyone (unconscious competence).

Another way to reflect on your performance is to use the Johari window (named after American psychologists Joseph Luft and Harry Ingham). A simple version is displayed below.

	Things I know	Things I don't know
Things they know	A Good at timekeeping Using my initiative	B
Things they don't know	C Going to bed late Behind with coursework	D

You may wish to draw your own. 'They' can be anyone relevant to the situation. In this example we will use your placement supervisor to mean 'they'.

In Box A put the things you know about yourself and others know. You may be good at timekeeping and using your initiative or common sense. In Box C put some things you know but others do not. You may go to bed too late and not get time to do your coursework. Sometimes people know things about you that you don't realise yourself. This is Box B. But how do you find out what you don't know? Simple – you ask!

This is a fun way to find out. In class, sit in a circle. Each person has a piece of paper and writes their name on the bottom like this:

Comment 1
Name – Joe Bloggs

Use a full A4 piece of paper, then pass it to the person on your left. They pass theirs to the left too. Your paper is now with the person next to you. They have to write a comment about you. Each person writes one comment at the top, then folds it over and passes it to the left. Eventually you will get your own paper back, folded over like a scroll.

You now have something to put in Box B. (Of course, to be really accurate it should go in Box A, but for now we'll keep it in Box B.)

Box D is the box for things you don't know and others don't know. This is how you react in a crisis. Perhaps Mrs Green starts to choke and you save her using your first aid training, or you have to deal with an angry relative and you do it calmly. Only when the unexpected happens do you and others realise you have hidden depths. Box D is for these unexpected qualities you have.

So how can this help you improve your performance? Look at Box B. Is there anything you could improve on? Do you need a reality check? Does anything surprise you? Perhaps you thought you were quiet but others find you noisy. Thinking about how you appear to others can help you to reflect on your own performance.

As you reflect on your work skills, your confidence will improve. Your log book should be a record of your development on a regular basis – not something to fill in at the last minute. Make your own checklist if your log book hasn't got one. How do you rate yourself at the start of the placement and then again at the end of the placement on the following?

Remember

When you do this the first time have a rule that all the comments should be positive ones! Later, when you know the people in your class, you may wish to give one positive comment and one thing to work on.

	Start of placement		End of placement	
	Good	Need to improve	Good	Need to improve
timekeeping				
confidence				
initiative				
ability to follow instructions				
strengths				
weaknesses				
career development plans				
progression opportunities				
activities undertaken and knowledge and skills gained				

Activity 22

Towards P5, D1, D2.
Complete a log book or placement diary using Gibbs's Reflective Cycle. Review your performance on this placement and reflect how you could improve on it. Use any feedback you have from placement to help you with this. What were the benefits to you? What were the benefits to placement of you being there?
Evaluate your work experience placement in terms of benefits to yourself and the placement. What did you gain from this placement? What did they gain by having you there?

Reflect on your personal attributes and how well suited you are to a career in health and social care.

SUMMARY

After working through this unit you should know how to:

- apply for a voluntary placement

- prepare and practise for a job interview

- use interpersonal skills in the care setting

- reflect on the skills and the knowledge you have gained

- complete a minimum of 60 hours in a health or social care setting.

Grading grid

In order to pass this unit, the evidence that the learner presents for assessment needs to demonstrate that they can meet all of the learning outcomes for the unit. The criteria for a pass grade describe the level of achievement required to pass this unit.

Grading criteria

To achieve a pass grade the evidence must show that the learner is able to:	To achieve a merit grade the evidence must show that, in addition to the pass criteria, the learner is able to:	To achieve a distinction grade the evidence must show that, in addition to the pass and merit criteria, the learner is able to:
P1 use two different methods to present personal information for placement application	**M1** describe strengths and weaknesses of own interpersonal skills as demonstrated on the work experience placement	**D1** evaluate own work experience placement in terms of benefits to self and the placement
P2 use appropriate interview skills for a health or social care work experience placement	**M2** reflect on and review own performance on placement	**D2** reflect on own personal attributes in relation to a career in health and social care
P3 complete a period of work experience in a health or social care setting		
P4 demonstrate the use of effective interpersonal skills on work experience		
P5 carry out a health and safety survey of a local environment used by a specific patient/service user group		

Cultural Diversity in Health and Social Care

Workers in health and social care need to understand the variety and diversity in British society today. We are not all the same and we do not all have the same beliefs or attitudes to events. Good quality services should provide for all, not just for a certain few. Individuals have rights and the healthcare worker has a duty to promote those rights, whether they agree with them or not.

This unit explores:

- the wide range of religious and secular (non-religious) beliefs and cultural differences
- the value of having a diverse society
- how knowledge of diversity can help make sure people have equal opportunities or chances in health and social care.

The unit also introduces you to the idea of rights balanced by responsibilities. Health and social care staff have rights and responsibilities. Patients and those who use social care services have rights and responsibilities too. The law dictates what rights people have in health and social care and in this unit we look at some of these laws.

This unit links very closely with *Unit 1: Communication and Individual Rights within the Health and Social Care Sectors* and gives a useful introduction to work in health and social care and a basis for progression to the Level 3 BTEC National Diploma. It may provide evidence for key skills Level 2 communication, information and communication technology, and improving own learning and performance.

Learning Outcomes

On completion of this unit you should be able to:

1 Explore the diversity of individuals in society
2 Examine practices in different religious or secular beliefs
3 Investigate factors that influence the equality of opportunity for individuals in society
4 Examine the rights of individuals in health and social care environments.

KEY TERMS

Diversity means 'variety'.

1 Explore the diversity of individuals in society

What if . . .

- we all had to wear the same clothes?
- we all had the same hairstyle?
- we all had to eat the same food?
- we all had to live in the same type of house?
- we all had to have the same size family?

Just imagine not being able to choose what you wear or how you look or what you eat. In some countries people are not allowed to have more than one child. In other countries people are not allowed to say what they think.

British society is not like this. It allows people to choose what to wear, how to live their lives, within reason, provided they stay within the law. This is why our society is so varied or diverse.

Social and political diversity

Social refers to how people behave and interact. Social diversity refers to the different ways in which people behave towards each other. Some people respect and help older people. Some people think old people are 'past it' and should be pensioned off. This is an example of differences in beliefs. This translates into differences in behaviour, so a person who respects older people will listen to them. A person who does not respect older people will not listen to their views.

Politics refers to how we are governed. Political diversity is another way of saying differences in how we choose to be governed, what laws we should have and what plans should be made for the people in our country. Political diversity in this country ranges from left wing to right wing.

Left-wing views	Right-wing views
The state should:	People should:
<ul><li>organise benefits for those too sick to work</li><li>help the unemployed with benefits</li><li>provide free health care</li><li>provide free education</li><li>provide a stock of council houses for people to rent.</li></ul>	<ul><li>have a private pension for when they are sick</li><li>find another job if they are made unemployed</li><li>pay for their own health care</li><li>pay for a good education</li><li>buy their own house.</li></ul>

Activity 1

What do you think – left wing or right wing?
Discuss the points in your group and decide whether you are left wing or right wing.

You probably found it hard to agree because you thought differently. This shows the diversity in your group. We can have different views because we have political diversity in our society. If we lived in a country where there was no choice and we were not allowed to discuss these matters, there would be less open political diversity. (People might still think differently but be frightened to express their views in case they were arrested and imprisoned for saying what they thought.)

Did you know?

Nelson Mandela was charged with trying to overthrow the government of South Africa. He was imprisoned for 18 years on Robben Island because he wanted black and white people to have the same opportunities in South Africa. He said in his defence: 'I have cherished the ideal of a democratic and free society in which all persons live together in harmony and with equal opportunities.'

Nelson Mandela

In our society we have diversity in

- ethnicity
- religious beliefs
- secular beliefs
- social class
- gender
- sexuality
- age
- family structure
- disabilities.

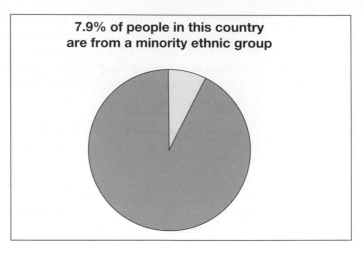

Ethnicity: population size

Source: National Statistics website: www.statistics.gov.uk. Crown copyright material is reproduced with the permission of the Controller of HMSO.

Ethnicity means ethnic group. It is sometimes used to refer to culture, or race or nationality. In fact, it is a term which changes its meaning. An ethnic group often defines itself by a common language or cultural heritage.

	Total population		Minority ethnic population
	Count	%	%
White	54153898	92.1	n/a
Mixed	677117	1.2	14.6
Asian or Asian British			
Indian	1053411	1.8	22.7
Pakistani	747285	1.3	16.1
Bangladeshi	283063	0.5	6.1
Other Asian	247664	0.4	5.3
Black or Black British			
Black Caribbean	565876	1.0	12.2
Black African	485277	0.8	10.5
Black other	97585	0.2	2.1
Chinese	247403	0.4	5.3
Other	230615	0.4	5.0
All minority ethnic population	*4635296*	*7.9*	*100*
All population	58789194	100	n/a

The UK population: by ethnic group, April 2001. The size of the minority ethnic population was 4.6 million in 2001 or 7.9 per cent of the total population of the United Kingdom.

Source: National Statistics website: www.statistics.gov.uk. Crown copyright material is reproduced with the permission of the Controller of HMSO.

The Office for National Statistics in the UK uses the following ethnic groups – white, mixed, Asian or Asian British, Black or Black British, Chinese and other. The groups have been subdivided into other ethnic groups so Asian or Asian British include Indian, Pakistani and Bangladeshi. See the table of results from the 2001 census opposite. Looking at the table, which group is the largest minority group? Which is second largest?

Did you find the Indian group is the largest ethnic minority, then the Pakistani group? The third largest group is the mixed ethnicity group.

One of the problems with using ethnicity as a term is that it makes some false assumptions. Not everyone from India speaks the same language – there are over 14 official state languages. India was a collection of different states ruled by the British until 1947. There is not one religion but many – Indian Christians, Indian Sikhs, Indian Hindus, Indian Buddhists, Indian Jains, Indian Muslims and many more. So you can see that the 'ethnic group' of Indians does not share a common language or religion. There is huge variety in food and customs between the people of north India and people from southern India too. You might almost think that the 'ethnic group' of Indians has very little in common with each other; nevertheless we classify Indians together for convenience when collecting information. In reality Indians are very diverse.

Religious beliefs vary in society. Some people believe in one God and some believe in many. Atheists do not believe in God at all. Agnostics say we cannot know if God exists because we cannot prove whether there is a God or not. Some people are Pagans.

KEY TERMS

Ethics means values (do not mix it up with ethnic).

Secular beliefs are non-religious beliefs. Most state schools in this country are secular – not religious. There are religious schools but not in the main state system. Health care is secular – not linked to religion. The police force is a secular organisation in this country and is not linked to religion. Humanists are secular. They believe that we are rational and logical beings who have the right and the responsibility to decide our own lives and shape our own society based on the ethics of human values. In our society we believe in not judging people before we have evidence to prove they are guilty. This is an ethical view, not linked to any religion.

Social class is one way people differ in British society. We class people according to their job, wealth, power and education, how they dress and how they behave. A hospital doctor would have a higher social class than a factory worker because they have a longer education and have better career prospects. In the long term they may earn a lot more and be able to afford a better house and better education for their children. Many people disagree with having social differences based on money and education but such differences still exist in our society.

The Office for National Statistics uses the following social and economic classification:

1   Higher managerial and professional occupations.
2   Lower managerial and professional occupations.
3   Intermediate occupations.
4   Small employers and own account workers.
5   Lower supervisory and technical occupations.
6   Semi-routine occupations.

7   Routine occupations.

8   Long-term unemployed (including those who have never worked).

Why does social class matter to some people? In this country social class is linked to health. According to the 2001 census, the higher class you are, the healthier you are likely to be. People in the lowest classes are more likely to have long-term illness or disability. This is not deliberately planned to be so, but it happens.

Activity 2

Look at the information about long-term illness and disability. Why do you think that the routine and the semi-routine workers suffer more long-term illness than higher professionals? (Routine occupations include factory workers and manual workers.)

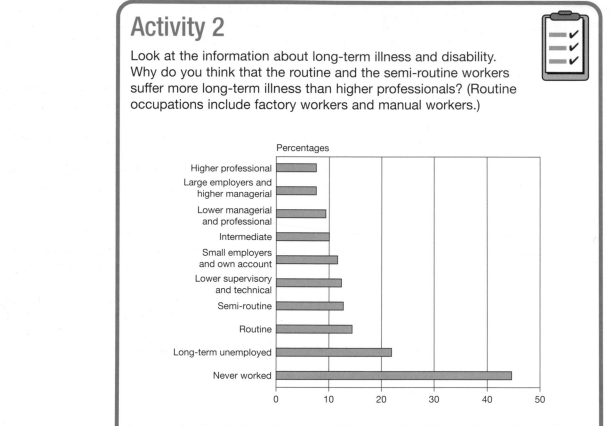

Age-standardised rates of long-term illness or disability which restricts daily activities: by NS-SEC, April 2001, England and Wales.

Source: National Statistics website: www.statistics.gov.uk. Crown copyright material is reproduced with the permission of the Controller of HMSO.

The government is concerned that there is such a difference in our society. Many government policies or plans aim to make things more equal. Working family tax credits are designed to help low-income families afford better food and a healthier lifestyle.

Did you know?

There are differences in social class on the Internet. Researcher Danah Boyd of the University of California has found social class divides between users of Facebook and MySpace. Facebook was originally limited to university students or those with an academic email address. Anyone could join MySpace. In the US military, officers are mostly on Facebook, while ordinary soldiers tend to use MySpace.

Gender or sexual category provides one aspect of our diverse society. People are male or female. Sometimes people are transgender and have to decide which gender they feel most comfortable with. According to the Women and Equality unit publication, *Gender Reassignment – a guide for employers 2005*, in the UK 5,000 people have gender reassignment and sometimes need surgery to help them belong to one gender (*source*: www.womenandequalityunit.gov.uk/).

Sexuality refers to a person's sexual preference. Gay and lesbian couples now have rights to enter into a civil partnership which is legally recognised.

Age is another source of diversity in our society. There are fewer children being born. At the same time people are living longer. This means that the population is ageing. The number of people over 85 is the fastest-growing sector. The UK population aged 85 or over more than doubled from 0.9 per cent in 1971 to 1.9 per cent in 2004.

Family structure is now more diverse – 24 per cent or nearly one in four families is a lone-parent family. Fewer children live in families with two parents. At the same time, more people are living alone – 7 million people lived alone in 2005.

Disabilities bring diversity too. The most common disability in under-20-year-olds is now asthma. Autism and autistic spectrum disorders and behavioural disorders are the main causes of severe disability. Statistics show that children of semi-skilled manual workers are more likely to have disabilities.

Activity 3

Towards P1.
Make an annotated poster to describe social and political factors that make people different from each other. Remember to include social factors such as ethnicity, religious beliefs, secular beliefs, social class, gender, sexuality, age, family structure, disabilities. Don't forget to include political differences. Give examples with your descriptions.

Range of religious groups/secular beliefs

In British society today there is a range of religious groups. This has often been the case in Britain. The Romans brought a variety of religions when they conquered Britain. The Vikings too had different religions. King Henry VIII invented the Church of England so that he could divorce his first wife. British society is as diverse as the rest of the world, but you may be surprised to learn which religions are closest to each other in beliefs.

Catholics, Muslims, Buddhists and Sikhs use prayer beads or rosaries to help them count their prayers

Did you know?

According to the *Encyclopedia Britannica 2005*, the largest three religious groups in the world are the Abrahamic religions – 53.5 per cent, Indian religions – 19.7 per cent and irreligious groups – 14.3 per cent.

Jews, Christians and Muslims all believe in the prophet Abraham and together they make up the Abrahamic religions. Hindus, Jains, Buddhists and Sikhs have similar beliefs in respecting others and doing good deeds in the world. These four religions make up the group of Indian religions. Irreligious groups are made up of free thinkers, humanists, agnostics, who say we can never prove whether there is a God, and atheists, who do not believe in God. All these religions and more are present in British society today.

2 Examine practices in different religious or secular beliefs

Why do we need to know about different religions? Isn't it enough to know about our own? If we only know about our own religion we may not understand the needs of others.

What's in a name? Have you ever heard someone ask a Jew or a Hindu person for their Christian name? Only Christians have Christian names. Jews have Jewish names. Hindus have Hindu names. Everyone has a first name.

How could the question have been asked? They could ask for their first name. This covers every religion and makes sure we get accurate information. This is just one example of why we need to know about practices in other religions and in non-religious beliefs. Some names associated with religions have special meanings. See the examples in the box below.

Christian names	Jewish names	Muslim names
Christian – follower of Christ Peter – a rock or stone John – God is gracious Kathleen – pure Felicity – happy	David – beloved Joshua – God rescues Daniel – God is my judge Deborah – a bee Rachel – purity Naomi – beautiful	Muhammad – praiseworthy Abdullah – servant of God Rahim – merciful, kind Salma – peaceful Nadia – the first Maryam – the name of the mother of Jesus

Does your name have a meaning? Is it linked to any religion? Perhaps you are Christian yet find your name is listed as Jewish. This is because the Jewish religion is much older than Christianity, but Christians share many beliefs with Jews. Jesus Christ was a Jew. He meant to improve the Jewish religion, but his followers started Christianity as an offshoot from the Jewish religion. Christians have the Bible, which is made up of the Old Testament Jewish books, and the New Testament Christian books. This is why Christians use Jewish names such as Sarah and Elizabeth.

Later still the Muslim religion was founded by the prophet Mohammad who was trying to get people to lead better lives. The Muslim religion is sometimes called Islam. Islam includes the beliefs of the Jewish and Christian religions. Islam has the same prophets – Abraham, Moses, Isaac and Jesus. Muslims believe that Mohammad also was given the word of God just as these others were. Some Muslim names are almost the same as Jewish or Christian names – Musa in Islam is the Jewish name Moses; Ibrahim in Islam is the same as Abraham in the Jewish and Christian religions.

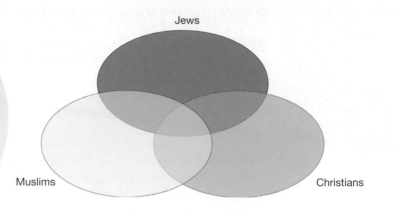

The Abrahamic religions share some common beliefs

Range of religious groups/secular beliefs

The figure below shows the religions in Britain in 2001.

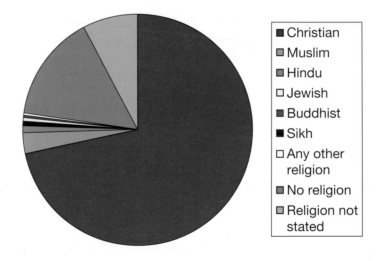

Christian
Muslim
Hindu
Jewish
Buddhist
Sikh
Any other religion
No religion
Religion not stated

Religions in Britain

Source: National Statistics website: www.statistics.gov.uk. Crown copyright material is reproduced with the permission of the Controller of HMSO.

Christians

The cross is important to Christians because Jesus died after being nailed to a cross (crucified). Most people in this country are Christians. This might seem straightforward, but there are many types of Christians and they do not all have the same customs or practices.

Christian symbol – the cross

Jehovah's Witnesses are a type of Christian. They are evangelical, which means they try to convert people to their religion. They believe the world will end soon. They do not accept that Jesus died on a cross, but think he died on a stake or pole. They do not accept the Holy Trinity of Jesus and God and the Holy Spirit.

Activity 4

Work with a partner and list as many religions as you can, then try to sort out which are Christian and which are not. Compare your list with the list below.
Here are some Christian religions:

- Roman Catholic
- Protestant
- Church of England
- Church of Scotland
- Methodist
- Quaker
- Seventh Day Adventists
- Salvation Army
- Eastern Orthodox
- Amish
- Christadelphians.

The Menorah is one of the oldest symbols in the Jewish religion. It symbolises the light and the example that Jews should set for others.

Jews

There are Orthodox Jews and Reform Jews. There are 13 principles of Jewish beliefs:

1 God exists.
2 God is unique.
3 God is intangible, not a person or thing.
4 God is eternal.
5 We should only pray to God.
6 The words of the prophets are true.
7 Moses was the greatest of the prophets.
8 The first five books of the Bible, the written Torah, and the oral Torah, which is in the Talmud, were given to Moses by God.
9 There is no other Torah.
10 God knows the thoughts and deeds of men.
11 God will reward the good and punish the wicked.
12 The Messiah or saviour will come.
13 The dead will be resurrected.

Moslems

The crescent moon symbolises Islam. The Islamic months are based on the phases of the moon.

Moslems are also called Muslims. The religion is Islam. There are two branches of Islam – the Sunni (said like 'sunny') and the Shiite (said 'shee – ite'). They have similar beliefs but have different views about who should have succeeded the prophet Mohammad.

The Five Pillars of Islam are the five things a Muslim should do. They are:

- Shahadah: sincerely reciting the Muslim profession of faith.
- Salat: performing ritual prayers in the proper way five times each day.
- Zakat: paying a charity tax to the poor.
- Sawm: fasting during the month of Ramadan.
- Hajj: pilgrimage to Mecca.

Jews, Christians and Muslims form the Abrahamic religions. Buddhists, Hindus and Sikhs are part of the Indian tradition of religions.

Buddhists

The Buddhist symbol

There are subdivisions of Buddhism. Southern Buddhism is found in Sri Lanka, Thailand and Myanmar. Eastern and Northern Buddhism are the other main types.

The Buddhist symbol of the eightfold path stands for:

- Right view – accepting the world as it is.
- Right intentions – being open and honest.
- Right speech – being genuine in what we say.
- Right discipline – simplicity in what we do.
- Right livelihood – accepting the job we do.
- Right effort – working to the best of our ability.
- Right mindfulness – precision in what we do.
- Right concentration – being focused on what we do.

Hindus

The Hindu god Shiva is one aspect of the one god Brahma. Shiva as Lord of Dance controls the movement of the universe.

Hindus believe in one god, Brahma, who created the universe, but worship other aspects such as Shiva, the destroyer and renewer of life, and Vishnu, the preserver and protector of life. Brahma, Vishnu and Shiva form a trinity. (This is a bit like the Christian idea of a Holy Trinity of Father, Son and Holy Spirit.)

Sikhs

The five Ks symbolise the Sikh religion and all Sikhs aim to maintain the five Ks:

- Kesh – uncut hair.
- Kara – a steel bracelet.
- Kanga – a wooden comb.
- Kaccha – a cotton undergarment.
- Kirpan – a ceremonial sword which can be a few inches long or a full-size sword.

Male Sikhs are often called Singh, which means 'lion'. Women do not change their name after marriage. Many Sikh women are called Kaur, which means 'princess'.

Rastafarians

Rastafarians originally believed that Emperor Haile Selassie of Ethiopia was a god and one day people of African origin would be returned to Ethiopia. They use marijuana and reggae music in worship sessions. Many Rastafarians do not cut their hair but instead have dreadlocks. There is no fixed belief as such but music and smoking marijuana are common bonds.

Atheists

Atheists do not believe in a God or gods. They believe that rational thought is the basis of life. There are several types of atheist, but most reject supernatural causes for events.

Humanists

Humanists are often classed with atheists but humanists have a positive approach to life. They believe that each individual should make the best of their life and that rational, logical thought provides a moral code to live by.

Pagans

There are several beliefs which come under the name of Paganism. Ancient religions such as the Druids and Wiccans were in this country before Christianity. The Druids used mistletoe as part of their ceremonies. Today we use mistletoe at Christmas. Wiccan is another name for witchcraft. Most pagan religions believe Nature is sacred. Some believe in spirits. Shamans believe in contacting spirits for guidance and advice. Sacred Ecologists, Odinists and Heathens are also part of the pagan community.

Beliefs/practices

There are many different types of religions. Within any one religion there are variations in beliefs, forms of worship and festivals.

In this section we will begin to look at some of those beliefs and practices, but this is only an introduction. You may wish to find out more about a particular religion or belief. Perhaps you already know about your own religion. If not, this may be a chance to learn! Use the chart on the following pages as a starting point.

Religion	Beliefs	Forms of worship	Festivals	Diet	Health/medical beliefs
Christians	One God in three aspects – Father, Son, Holy Spirit	Pray in church on Sunday. Some believe that bread and wine become the body and blood of Christ at Mass	Christmas – birth of Christ, 25 December for some, 6 January for Eastern Orthodox Christians Easter – the death and coming to life again of Christ Pentecost – similar to Jewish Shavuot, celebrates the Holy Spirit	They eat meat and fish. They give up some food as part of fasting at Lent	Some Christians do not drink alcohol
Jehovah's Witnesses	One God	Form part of a tight community but spend time trying to convert others	They do not celebrate Christmas or Easter, but remember the anniversary of Christ's death	No tea, coffee or alcohol	No blood transfusions allowed
Jews	One God	The Sabbath begins at nightfall on Friday and lasts until nightfall on Saturday	Hanukkah, the Jewish Festival of Lights Passover – commemorates when the Jews were led out of Egypt by Moses Yom Kippur – the most sacred day. There are other holy days	No pork Meat should be killed so it is kosher. Dairy and meat foods are separated	Towels are separate for different parts of the body
Moslems	One God	Pray five times a day, usually in a mosque Give money to the poor	Eid ul Fitr, which marks the end of Ramadan Eid ul Adha remembers the prophet Ibrahim's obedience to God in being willing to sacrifice his own son. At this Eid wealthy people have a sheep or cow slaughtered to feed the poor	No pork No alcohol Meat should be killed so it is Halal	Fasting in the month of Ramadan is good for the body and for the soul
Buddhists	Focus on spiritual	Use mantras and prayer wheels to aid	Wesak, the most important festival, is at the full moon in May. It	Vegetarian	Acceptance of what happens reduces

	God	Worship	Festivals	Diet	Beliefs/values
	development. Do not worship gods	concentration. Use meditation to achieve a higher state of spirituality	celebrates the Buddha's birthday. There are many more festivals		stress. All things pass. Meditation helps focus on the important things, not material things
Hindus	One God, Brahma, and three aspects of that God. Many deities which are aspects of Brahma	Individual worship at home as well as at the temple. Offerings made to deities	Diwali, the Hindu festival of lights, is also celebrated by Jains and Sikhs. Vaisakhi – people go to the temple and exchange gifts and sweets between friends and family members	Mostly vegetarian. No beef at all, even if they eat meat	What we do in this life influences how we experience the next life. If we suffer now, we must have done something wrong in a previous life
Sikhs	One god	Individual prayer and group worship at a Gurdwara. No images used in worship	Vaisakhi – the Sikh New Year festival April 13–14. Diwali celebrates the release from prison of the sixth guru, in 1619. Hola Mohalla, Sikhs hold mock battles	Sometimes but not always vegetarian. Occasionally eat eggs and chicken	All people are equal and we should help each other. No alcohol or tobacco as they are not good for the body. What we do in this life affects the next life
Atheists	No god	Personal choice	No festivals	Personal choice	Personal responsibility
Humanists	No god – just human reason	Personal choice	No festivals	Personal choice	Personal responsibility
Rastafarians	Emperor Haile Selassie of Ethiopia is a god	Group music session, Nyabingi, and smoking marijuana to help meditation	Ethiopian Christmas (7 January), crowning of Emperor Haile Selassie I (2 November), many others	Vegetarian. Live close to Nature, simple diet	Women are not equal to men. No contraception or abortion
Pagans	Many spirits or gods in Nature	Various, usually related to Nature	Eight festivals – based on Celtic festivals and the solar calendar. Celebrations include Yuletide and midsummer		Live in harmony with Nature, men and women equally important

There are many other aspects of religions which we have no space to examine here. Customs relating to birth, marriage and death vary between religions.

Activity 5

Find out what customs there are around the birth of a child in your own religion, if you are religious, then compare with someone from a different religion. Some religions have a formal ceremony to welcome a child into a religion.

What happens when someone dies? Talk to people in your family and find out what customs there are. Are they based on religion or belief?

In many religions people are invited for a meal to remember the person who died. In Catholic Ireland it was the custom to sit all night with the body. In other religions it is the custom to bury the dead person as soon as possible. How might knowledge of these customs help you in caring for people from different backgrounds?

Marriage customs in Christianity, Judaism and Islam

Christian: Roman Catholic

Couples usually choose their own partners. They usually have to have some link with the church in which they wish to marry. It is more common now for Roman Catholics to marry non-Catholics. Marriage banns are declared, making the intended marriage public. This allows anyone to object to the marriage if they know of any legal reason why it should not happen. The couple have marriage preparation advice from the priest. Sometimes the bride gets together with her friends to enjoy their company before she is married. The groom may also spend time with his male friends.

The religious ceremony is held in Church in front of family and friends. It includes prayers and music and may include Mass. It must include an exchange of vows and rings. The bride is usually given away by her father or a male relative. She often wears white and may wear a veil. After the religious ceremony, the couple sign the register. In the Catholic religion, marriage is for having children, so contraception and abortion are not allowed. In the Catholic Church, marriage is for life, so divorce is not recognised by the Church.

Jewish

Marriage is sometimes arranged through parents and a matchmaker. The engagement marks the start of celebrations. The week before the wedding is Ufruf, when the groom announces the wedding. Sweets are thrown at him to celebrate. Mikveh is a purification ceremony for the bride. This includes a ritual bath. Some Mikvehs are like health clubs.

The contract (Ketubah) is signed before the ceremony and the man may also sign a Get, which says he will not contest a divorce if the woman wants a divorce later. The veiling ceremony occurs when the groom puts a veil over the bride. This shows he will clothe her.

Her father or both parents lead her to the Chupa, which signifies the couple's home. She enters the Chupa last and walks round the groom. Orthodox Jews walk round seven times to signify building a new home. Seven glasses of wine are drunk to remember the seven days in which God created the world. The groom gives the bride a ring, which is a perfect unbroken circle signifying harmony in marriage. At the end of the ceremony, a glass is broken to remind people of the destruction of the Temple thousands of years ago. The ceremony does not have to be in a synagogue.

Muslim

In Islam, marriage is a social contract with rights and obligations on both sides. If the contract is broken, either person can ask for a divorce. Parents see it as their duty to get their children married, and marriage is regarded as the ideal state. They may look for a suitable match for their son or daughter or may ask a friend to act as matchmaker. A good match is usually someone who has similar religious beliefs and a similar background. It is important that women are taken care of. Couples usually meet before the marriage to make sure they like each other, but sex before marriage is not allowed.

According to the Koran, Muslim men may have up to four wives at one time, provided they can care equally for each and give each one the same standard of living. The wife must agree to this. A Muslim is not allowed to hurt another Muslim so cannot take another wife without his first wife's consent. A Muslim woman may have only one husband at a time, but may marry again after a divorce. In this country the law says people can have only one husband or wife at a time, so second or later wives are not legally recognised if the first wife is still married to the man. It is thought that the tradition of having four wives arose when women who had no husband had no protection in society. Men were encouraged to take more wives to protect the women. This is still the case in some countries today, such as Afghanistan.

The wedding contract does not require the bride to be present but she must give her consent to the marriage. Sometimes the contract is signed and witnessed many months before the couple live together. It is forbidden for anyone to trick or force people into marriage in Islam.

On marriage, the groom must give the bride a present of money. This is the Mahr, which she keeps for herself. If she later divorces her husband against his will, she returns the Mahr. If they divorce by mutual consent or against her wishes, she keeps the Mahr. If a woman has money of her own, it remains her own. Her husband is obliged to keep and support her and any children they have. A wife is entitled to keep any money she earns for herself.

The Muslim wedding is possibly the simplest of ceremonies. It is called a Nikah. The bride does not have to be present if she sends two witnesses. There is a reading from the Koran and an exchange of vows in front of witnesses. All Muslim marriages have to be declared publicly. Sometimes hundreds of people are invited to a Walimah and the bride and groom sit on a raised area so everyone can see them. The Walimah is not compulsory.

Cultural variations occur just as they do in Christian weddings. In some countries, marriage involves the exchange of gifts between the two families. Wealthy families take the opportunity to show off their wealth, although this is not in accordance with Islamic ideas. Sometimes there is a ceremony where the bride is made beautiful by her friends using henna to create patterns on the hands and feet. The bride may wear red – the traditional colour for brides in India. (In some Asian countries, white is used for mourning or for older people, so white is not often used for brides.) These cultural variations are nothing to do with the Muslim religion.

Activity 6

Towards P2.
Compare the practices and beliefs of individuals from two contrasting religious groups/secular beliefs. You may wish to produce an illustrated booklet using your ICT skills.

3 Investigate factors that influence the equality of opportunity for individuals in society

We have seen the variety of religious and non-religious beliefs there is in Britain today. People's beliefs influence the opportunities they have. A Rastafarian woman may not have the same chances as a Rastafarian man. A Sikh woman may have the same opportunities as a Sikh man in her own community. But what happens when people move outside their close communities? Other factors then influence the equality of opportunities. In this next section we will examine what factors influence life chances and how they do so.

Social and political factors

Whether people have the same chances as others depends a lot on the following factors:

- ethnicity
- religious beliefs
- social class
- gender
- sexuality
- age
- family structure
- disabilities.

Ethnicity as we saw earlier is not easy to define, but we do know that in 2001 only 7.9 per cent of the British population was from an ethnic minority; 92.1 per cent of people were from the ethnic majority. In reality the bigger or more dominant a group, the more that services cater for them. So job adverts are written in the dominant language – English. If someone cannot speak or read or write English they have difficulty in getting work.

Religious beliefs can limit opportunities. A Buddhist is not likely to work in a slaughterhouse killing animals. A Pagan who believes in being close to Nature is unlikely to settle in a city job. A Muslim who wishes to pray five times a day may face difficulty when they need the time away from the factory floor.

Social class is one of the main factors which limit opportunity in this country, because social class influences the amount of education and wealth a family has. Children go to school in their local area, but where they live is determined by where they can afford. Those living on a council estate may go to the local school. Those who own their own house may choose to live near a school which has better results so their children can have a better education. A better education gives more choice of jobs.

Gender influences job opportunities and whether a person is willing to take the chances they are offered. Some jobs such as care work are dominated by one gender – only 10 per cent of nurses are men. Some women who are mothers leave nursing because they find it difficult to manage childcare responsibilities with long working hours.

Sexuality may influence the opportunities people are given. According to a report by Stonewall (www.stonewall.org.uk), 75 per cent of young gay people attending a faith school have been bullied and 97 per cent hear insulting remarks about gay people. Over half of gay and lesbian pupils feel unable to be themselves at school.

Age is a factor in whether people are given the same chances as others. People used to be discriminated against because they were seen as too young or too old for certain jobs. Older people were made to retire or were made redundant because of their age. Young people were told they did not have experience.

Family structure influences life chances. A single parent bringing up children will struggle to find the money for school trips or school uniform. According to a Labour Force Survey, in the three months to June 2007, 57.1 per cent of lone parents with young children were employed, compared with 71.1 per cent of married or cohabiting mothers (*source*: http://www.statistics.gov.uk).

Disabilities may be physical or mental. Mental illness is a factor in how people experience opportunities. In a study of people with psychotic mental illness, in 2000, Maureen O'Brien found that 70 per cent of people with this mental illness were unemployed. Of those who did have jobs, half of them had part-time jobs. As a result they experienced money problems. The Equality and Human Rights Commission, which replaced the Commission for Racial Equality, the Disability Rights Commission and the Equal Opportunities Commission, explains the rights people have under the law (www.equalityhumanrights.com).

Discriminatory practice

Discriminatory practice means how people are discriminated against. It happens in four ways:

1 Prejudice – or prejudging people without really knowing them. A social worker may assume that all Asian families care for their old people, so Mrs Begum does not need home care.
2 Discrimination – favouring one person over another one, or being against someone for no reason. A GP receptionist may think that anyone over 50 can have a daytime appointment because the assumption is that they do not work.
3 Stereotyping – classifying someone without really seeing them as a person. An Afro-Caribbean man in casualty may be stereotyped as a porter, when he may in fact be a doctor.
4 Labelling – seeing only one part of a person, seeing their colour or disability rather than the whole person. A person using a walking stick may be labelled as needing help but they may be perfectly independent.

Activity 7

Case Study

Jared is 16 and lives in care. He comes to college. He is mixed race. Some of the other students get to know he is in care and start talking about him in the refectory. 'He must have done something wrong to be in care,' Sarah says. 'I'm not going to be friends with him – I don't want to mix with people like that. My dad says all the kids from that area are gangsters or druggies.' As Jared comes in they all go quiet. When he comes over they all look away and Jane puts her bag on the seat so he cannot sit with them. Later Sarah's boyfriend and some mates wait for Jared and push him around as he walks to the bus stop.

How is Sarah prejudging Jared?
How is she stereotyping Jared?
How is she labelling him?
Who is discriminating and how are they doing it?

Effects of discrimination on the individual

When people are discriminated against it may affect them in the following ways:

● **P**hysical
● **I**ntellectual
● **E**motional
● **S**ocial.

Think of **PIES** as a way to remember these four things.

The effects on Jared might be:

- Physical – being pushed around now might lead to him being beaten up later.
- Intellectual – he might not want to come to class as the others are so unfriendly.
- Emotional – he may feel upset or scared and become withdrawn and depressed.
- Social – he may be lonely as everyone avoids him because they want to be friends with Sarah and her crowd.

Examples of non-discriminatory practice

In health and social care we must not be like Sarah in the case study. We should see people as individuals.

Individual worker responsibilities

The individual worker is responsible for their own actions. In health and social care you can never say 'I did it because s/he told me to.' If you hurt someone, you made that choice and you have to take responsibility for it. If you see discrimination, never join in. Ask why the person discriminating thinks the way they do and ask them to see the person as an individual, not a stereotype. Discrimination is never acceptable in care. Challenge it and try to get it stopped.

Institutional responsibilities

Institutions such as care homes, day centres, hospitals and educational establishments have a 'duty of care' to protect people. There must be equal opportunities policies to guide staff how to behave. The manager in charge must make sure all staff have training on providing care which sees the person first and does not stereotype. The staff then have individual responsibility to make sure they treat people fairly. The manager must have a complaints procedure so that anyone who feels they have been discriminated against can complain and have that complaint carefully investigated.

Working with colleagues

Not discriminating and treating people fairly extends to the people you work with. In health and social care, people must respect service users and also everyone they work with. It is important not to prejudge colleagues and not to discriminate against them in any way. Male nurses should not be given tasks such as heavy lifting just because they are male. They should not have to have a chaperone when with patients if a female nurse does not have a chaperone with patients.

Working with patients/service users

When we are working with patients in health care and service users in social care we must not prejudge, stereotype, label or discriminate, but must treat each person as an individual and offer them the same opportunities. Always ask how a person would like to be addressed. Do not assume that because they are older they would like to be called Mr or Mrs. They may prefer to be called by their first name.

Materials

Equipment

The equipment we use must be suitable for all. The gown you offer a person in outpatients should be equally suitable for men and women. At a day centre there should be equipment that can be used by everyone, not just a few. Mugs should have easy-grip handles so people with arthritis can enjoy a mug of tea with everyone else without needing a 'special cup'.

Activities

The activities provided should be suitable for everyone or a choice of activities should be offered. Some men like knitting and some women like watching football or horse racing on television. In the care home, think of the people and their likes and dislikes. Don't assume you know – ask them! In the play corner of a nursery provide a variety of activities for boys and girls. Some girls like to play with cars and some boys like to play at cooking.

Visual displays

These should represent a variety of people, of different ethnic backgrounds and genders, so include male nurses and female doctors. The staff and service users of the day centre may well be from a variety of backgrounds and all should be represented.

Toys and books that provide positive images of gender and race should be part of the everyday equipment for children. Some useful books by Todd Parr that help children value themselves are *It's OK to be Different* and *The Family Book*. Avoid stereotypes in books. Another book which promotes diversity for children is *One Dad, Two Dads, Brown Dad, Blue Dads* by Johnny Valentine, illustrated by Melody Sarecky.

Activity 8

P3 – describe factors that may influence the equality of opportunities for individuals.
M1 – explain differences in health and social care service delivery necessary to promote equality of opportunity for individuals.
Base your answer on a case study of someone from a television programme or make up your own case study.

The role of the media

Our ways of thinking and behaving are formed by what we see around us. Sometimes we accept what we see without thinking but when we work in health and social care we need to ask why we think as we do. Sometimes we need to change.

Books can encourage discrimination or question it. *The Curious Incident of the Dog in the Night-time* by Mark Haddon is a very good book which tells the story from the viewpoint of someone with autism.

Leaflets sometimes stereotype people. Older people are shown as needing a stairlift or a hearing aid. Some young people may have hearing problems, but hearing aid advertisements use pictures of older people. **Newspapers** may stereotype people as 'thugs' or 'scroungers' because sensational headlines sell newspapers. **Magazines** show celebrities as people concerned with how they look. Some celebrities do a lot of good work but they don't get noticed for that. **Television** programmes often stereotype people as East End Cockneys or Australian surfers. Vicky Pollard is a stereotypical teenager from a poor part of town.

The Internet has opened up communication and possibilities for breaking down barriers between people. As it is not regulated it also opens up opportunities for prejudice and stereotyping. The individual has to choose how they use it. YouTube gives the opportunity to post a video. Geriatric 1927 is a retired person who has his own site and presents the point of view of an older person. The Zimmers, a group of older people, recorded a performance of The Who song 'My generation', which challenged stereotypical views of older people.

Did you know?

Media is the plural of medium.

Activity 9

Towards P4, M2, D1.

Case Study

Marge has lived in Sunnydale care home since her husband died. Marge trained as a concert pianist. Her mother was Russian. In the Second World War she worked as a translator because she was fluent in German and Russian. After the war she trained as a florist and grew her own plants in her garden.

In the care home, Marge is helped to wash and dress. After breakfast she sits in the lounge until lunchtime. The television is on most of the time. After lunch she sits in the lounge until tea time. In the evening the residents go to bed. Marge spends a lot of time thinking about her past life. An activities co-ordinator comes once a week to play bingo with the residents.

How could an understanding of diversity help promote Marge's rights?

What discriminatory practice can you see in this case study?

What could be done about it?

Explain the possible effects of discrimination on Marge's physical, intellectual, emotional and social health/wellbeing.

4 Examine the rights of individuals in health and social care environments

Responsibilities

In health and social care both employers and employees have responsibility to promote the rights of individuals. This is a 'duty of care'. Organisations which offer services such as health or social care are service providers.

Employers

Public authorities such as the NHS and social services departments must uphold and promote human rights in everything they do. They have legal duties relating to gender, race and disability.

Did you know?

Discrimination means refusing to provide a service, offering a lower standard of service or offering a service on different terms than you would to other people.

Did you know?

Any discrimination or harassment by an individual employee in the course of his or her employment is treated as also being committed by the employer and therefore both employee and employer are liable. The employer is legally liable even if they do not know it has happened.

Employers in hospitals, clinics, surgeries, day centres all have a duty to promote the rights of individuals. They do not have a choice. They must avoid discrimination in how they offer that service. They must not discriminate on any of the following grounds:

● disability
● gender
● race
● religion or belief
● sexual orientation.

110

Some exceptions

Very occasionally it is lawful to discriminate, for example single-sex clinics such as a 'Well Woman' clinic where it would be embarrassing for men to be present. The surgery can offer 'Well Man' clinics so no one is deprived of a service. Another example is that of a care home with limited parking space. Two spaces nearest the entrance are allocated for those with disabilities.

Employees

Employees working in health and social care must make sure they do not discriminate. As part of their induction, every care worker should have equal opportunities training and they must then practise this.

Individual rights

Individual rights are the rights of people who use health and social care services. They are rights given by law. These are the rights to:

- be respected
- be treated equally and not be discriminated against
- be treated as an individual
- be treated in a dignified way
- privacy
- be protected from danger and harm
- be cared for in the way that meets their needs, takes account of their choices and also protects them
- access information about themselves
- communicate using their preferred methods of communication and language.

Roles and impact of the following conventions, legislation and regulations

Conventions are laws which relate to several countries in a group. Individual countries ratify or sign up to the laws which cover their group. Sometimes individual countries decide not to ratify this law, which means they do not accept that law for their country.

The European Convention on Human Rights and Fundamental Freedoms 1950 bans torture and discrimination. Article 2 gives the right to life, and Article 5 gives the right to liberty and security. Under this Convention it is illegal to tie residents in chairs as a means of restraint as this denies them their liberty.

The Convention on the Rights of the Child 1989 includes rights to food, shelter, clean water, formal education and primary health care. There are rights which protect children from abuse, neglect, exploitation and cruelty. Other rights entitle children to express opinions and to have a say in matters affecting their life. Under this Convention children have a right to say who they prefer to live with if parents split up.

The Children Act 1989 brought together a lot of different laws about children, made local authorities responsible for fostering, child minding and day care as well as residential children's homes.

The Children Act 2004

Case Study: Victoria Climbie

Victoria Climbie died in hospital in 2000 with 128 different injuries to her body. She was eight years old, monitored by social services and cared for by her aunt and her aunt's boyfriend. Social workers did not realise she was not attending school. When she was admitted to hospital with broken bones, doctors did not know she was under the care of social services. They did not talk to each other and Victoria's aunt continued ill-treating her until she died from the abuse.

Everyone was appalled at how our society could fail to protect a vulnerable child. A government inquiry was held and several recommendations were made which eventually were formed into a policy called *Every Child Matters: Change for Children*. The aims of *Every Child Matters* are:

● be healthy
● stay safe
● enjoy and achieve
● make a positive contribution
● achieve economic wellbeing.

You can find out more on www.everychildmatters.gov.uk.

Every Child Matters then led to the Children Act 2004. The aim of the Children Act is to streamline services for children so that different organisations caring for children will see the whole picture. This will improve the overall service for children through joint planning, buying-in and delivery of services. This should make everyone more accountable for their part in planning and delivering care. This was needed because professionals did not talk to each other and children were not properly looked after. Local authorities now have a duty to promote the educational achievement of looked-after children. There is now a Children's Commissioner who represents the views of children.

The Mental Health Act 1983 provides for the compulsory detention and treatment in hospital of those with mental disorders. A person may be admitted to hospital under Part 2 of the Act if there is a formal application by either an Approved Social Worker (ASW) or the nearest relative. The application must be supported by recommendations made by two qualified medical practitioners, one of whom must be approved for the purpose under the Act. Patients may apply to a tribunal to be considered for discharge.

The Mental Capacity Act 2005 protects vulnerable people who are not able to make their own decisions. It makes clear who can take decisions, in which situations, and how they should go about this. It helps people to plan ahead for a time when they may lose the capacity to make their own decisions.

The Mental Health Act 2007 amends the Mental Health Act 1983 and gives people a right to an advocate when they are detained, and protects children from being put on adult wards inappropriately. There are new safeguards over the use of electro-convulsive therapy, for people detained under the Mental Capacity Act.

Activity 10

Use these websites to find out about the Mental Health Act:
http://www.mind.org.uk
http://www.mentalhealthalliance.org.uk.

Race Relations Act 1976, Race Relations (Amendment) Act 2000

The 1976 legislation made racial discrimination illegal. The 2000 amendment requires public bodies to promote race equality. Schools, local authorities and hospitals must all get rid of unlawful racial discrimination and promote equality of opportunity and good relations between people of different racial groups.

The Commission for Racial Equality (CRE) was set up to enforce the Race Relations Act. The CRE has now become part of the Equality and Human Rights Commission.

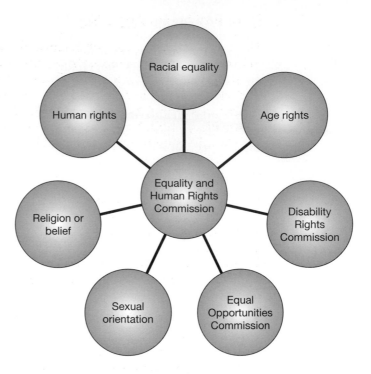

The Equality and Human Rights Commission (http://www.equalityhumanrights. com) acts for everyone in society and has new enforcement powers to guarantee people's equality. It must also promote understanding of the Human Rights Act. The Equality and Human Rights Commission is a non-departmental public body (NDPB) established under the Equality Act 2006 – accountable for its public funds, but independent of government.

Disability Discrimination Act 1995, Disability Discrimination Act 2005

After the 1995 Act, it became illegal to refuse a job to someone because they had a disability. The Act gave people with disabilities rights in:

- employment
- education
- access to goods and facilities
- buying land or property.

The 2005 Disability Discrimination Act extended the powers of the 1995 Act.

It became illegal for operators of public transport to discriminate against people with disabilities. This means that the rail service has to provide facilities so that disabled people can travel. This might mean ramps at stations or help from a guard. Buses now have lower platforms to enable people with disabilities to board. For the first time the definition of disability was extended to cover 'hidden' disabilities such as HIV, cancer and multiple sclerosis.

Data Protection Act 1998

The Data Protection Act 1998 replaced the 1984 Data Protection Act (see the Information Commissioner's Office website at www.ico.gov.uk). The Act applies to 'personal data', about identifiable living individuals, and covers both personal data held electronically and manual or paper data held in structured files or easily accessible systems. The Data Protection Act gives rights to individuals about whom information is held. It also requires those who record and use 'personal information' to follow the eight principles of good information handling.

Data must be:

- fairly and lawfully processed
- processed for limited purposes
- adequate, relevant and not excessive
- accurate
- not kept for longer than is necessary
- processed in line with the data subject's rights
- secure
- not transferred to countries without adequate protection.

Data may be processed only where the individual has given their consent. The Data Protection Act 1998 gives individuals the right of access to information held about them but forbids releasing that information to anyone else without permission, unless there is a legal requirement to do so.

Care Standards Act 2000, Nursing and Residential, Care Homes Regulations 1984 (amended 2002)

The Care Standards Act 2000 replaces previous legislation such as the Registered Homes Act 1984 and amendments. The Act established a new Commission for Social Care Inspection (CSCI) with powers to register, regulate and inspect:

- domiciliary social care providers
- independent fostering agencies
- residential family centres
- boarding schools
- residential care homes for adults
- nursing homes
- children's homes.

The 2000 Act stated what must be done. This was in contrast to the 1984 legislation which allowed flexibility of interpretation. The 2000 Act set out legally required national minimum standards. Some of these standards, such as minimum room size, were difficult for small homes to meet and thus many of them closed. Under the CSCI, inspectors are powerful. They can demand to see documents about the running of a home and talk to service users in private about the care they receive. You can find out about the work of the CSCI and read inspection reports for your area at www.csci.org.uk.

Human Rights Act 1998

Under the 1998 Act these are human rights:

- right to life
- protection from torture
- protection from slavery and forced labour
- right to liberty and security
- right to a fair trial
- no punishment without law
- right to respect for private and family life
- freedom of thought, belief and religion
- freedom of expression
- freedom of assembly and association
- right to marry
- protection from discrimination
- protection of property
- right to education
- right to free elections.

We all have a right to life, but under the Act we do not have a right to commit suicide or ask others to help us die.

Case Study

Pretty v United Kingdom (2002)

A woman suffering from a fatal disease wanted to control when and how she died. She did not want to die a slow and painful death and wanted her husband to help her die, but she did not want him to be accused of murder. The European Court of Human Rights found that the right to life does not give people a right to choose when and how they die.

Adapted from 'Human rights, human lives', Department for Constitutional Affairs, 2006.

The Human Rights Act 1998 gives individuals the right to challenge in the UK courts any actions or decisions of public authorities which they believe have violated their rights.

The Sex Discrimination Act was amended in May 1999 to protect transsexual people against discrimination in employment and vocational training.

Codes of practice and charters

Codes of practice are not the same as laws. A law is something everyone in the country must follow. Codes of practice apply to certain professions.

General Social Care Council/Care Council for Wales/Northern Ireland Social Care

The regulating body for social care workers is the General Social Care Council. It produces a code of practice for employers and one for social care workers. Social workers must register with the GSCC. If they break the code they may be removed from the register, which means they cannot work as a social worker, or they may be suspended for a period or given a public admonishment. You can read why people get removed from the register on the conduct section of the GSCC website. A social worker was recently removed from the register for breaking confidentiality and giving personal information to a third party who had no right to have it.

Activity 11

Towards P5, M3, D2.

Get a copy of the codes of conduct for employers and for social care workers at www.gscc.org.uk

How does the code for social care workers support the rights of individuals within a residential care home?

How effective is the code of practice in valuing diversity, promoting equality and supporting the rights of individuals in health and social care environments?

The Nursing and Midwifery Council has a code of conduct too which can be found on its website at www.nmc-uk.org.

The NMC code of professional conduct: standards for conduct, performance and ethics

As a registered nurse, midwife or specialist community public health nurse, you are personally accountable for your practice. In caring for patients and service users, you must:

- respect the patient or service user as an individual
- obtain consent before you give any treatment or care
- protect confidential information
- co-operate with others in the team
- maintain your professional knowledge and competence
- be trustworthy
- act to identify and minimise risk to patients and service users.

These are the shared values of all the United Kingdom healthcare regulatory bodies.

Source: www.nmc-uk.org.

Charters set out what should happen in good practice. A charter for deaf people with mental illness was written by the Mental Health Foundation and the charity, Sign, working together. It has a ten-point plan for what is needed. See it in full on http://www.deaf-friendly.org.uk/Deaf_Mental_Health_Charter.pdf.

Charters set out what is good practice and are often aimed at helping service users.

Organisation policies are written to help organisations comply with their legal duty. The Health and Safety at Work Act states the legal duty of employers and employees, but every care organisation must have a health and safety policy saying how they manage health and safety in their workplace. The Equality and Human Rights Commission enforce all the laws about equality, but every organisation must have a policy saying what they do about equality in their organisation. Policies interpret the law for that particular workplace or organisation.

Procedures specify how the policies are put into practice. An equal opportunities policy may say the organisation does not discriminate. The procedure says how this happens, so the procedure for placing a job advertisement may be that it does not ask for any specific gender or age of applicant. A social worker will explain the complaints procedure so service users know how to complain.

Laws change and policies should be revised as the law changes. Procedures may also need to change. It is not easy to keep up-to-date with changes in laws. Listen to the news and check the government website (www.direct.gov.uk) to keep up to speed.

Activity 12

Towards P5.
Describe one piece of relevant legislation and one code of practice or charter for a chosen health or social care environment that aims to support the rights of the individual.

One of the best sources for legislation on equality is the Equality and Human Rights Commission website at www.equalityhumanrights.com.

For the Children Act 2004 look at http://www.everychildmatters.gov.uk.

You may wish to use a code of practice from nursing or from social care. Alternatively you may wish to describe a charter.

M3 – explain how the legislation and code of practice/charter support the rights of individuals within the chosen environment.

Use the same legislation and code of practice or charter that you used in P5 and apply it to a care work situation.

Activity 12 (continued)

D2 – evaluate the effectiveness of the chosen legislation and code of practice/charter in valuing diversity, promoting equality and supporting the rights of individuals in health and social care environments.

How far do the law and the code of practice help in:

● valuing diversity?
● promoting equality?
● supporting the rights of individuals?

You must relate your answer to health and social care environments.

SUMMARY

● Our society is a rich tapestry of cultures and differences. Sexuality, age, family structure and difference in abilities all add to the diversity of society.

● Social class, education and wealth create further differences in society but everyone has a right to healthcare and social care.

Grading grid

In order to pass this unit, the evidence that the learner presents for assessment needs to demonstrate that they can meet all of the learning outcomes for the unit. The criteria for a pass grade describe the level of achievement required to pass this unit.

Grading criteria		
To achieve a pass grade the evidence must show that the learner is able to:	To achieve a merit grade the evidence must show that, in addition to the pass criteria, the learner is able to:	To achieve a distinction grade the evidence must show that, in addition to the pass and merit criteria, the learner is able to:
P1 describe social and political factors that make people different from each other	**M1** explain differences in health and social care service delivery necessary to promote equality of opportunity for individuals	**D1** explain the possible effects of discrimination on the physical, intellectual, emotional, and social health/wellbeing of individuals
P2 compare the practices and beliefs of individuals from two contrasting religious groups/secular beliefs	**M2** identify discriminatory practice and suggest how it can be avoided	**D2** evaluate the effectiveness of the chosen legislation and code of practice/charter in valuing diversity, promoting equality and supporting the rights of individuals in health and social care environments
P3 describe factors that may influence the equality of opportunities for individuals	**M3** explain how the legislation and code of practice/charter support the rights of individuals within the chosen environment	
P4 identify how understanding diversity can help promote the rights of patients/service users		
P5 describe one piece of relevant legislation and one code of practice or charter for a chosen health or social care environment that aims to support the rights of the individual		

Anatomy and Physiology for Health and Social Care

This unit provides knowledge and understanding about the way our bodies work. It looks at the systems within the body and the processes that are necessary to keep us alive. It also investigates potential malfunctions in the body (when the systems do not work correctly). The unit will also provide understanding about how to monitor body systems by recording routine measurements. We will also look at concepts of hazards and risk.

Learning Outcomes

On completion of this unit you should be able to:

1 Investigate the organisation of the human body
2 Understand the structure, function and interrelationship of major body systems
3 Investigate how monitoring body systems through routine measurements and observations can indicate malfunctions
4 Examine malfunctions in body systems and resultant needs of patients/ service users.

1 Investigate the organisation of the human body

All human bodies are made up of millions of cells and they all vary in size and shape depending on their function. A **cell** can only be seen under a microscope as it is incredibly small. However, all cells have:

● a **membrane** – this is a thin wall which holds in the cytoplasm. It also controls the substances which enter and leave the cell.
● **cytoplasm** – this is a jelly-like structure which provides energy to keep the cell alive. Chemical reactions take place here.
● a **nucleus** – this area controls cell division and is responsible for the function of the cell, e.g. a blood cell, a muscle cell or a nerve cell.

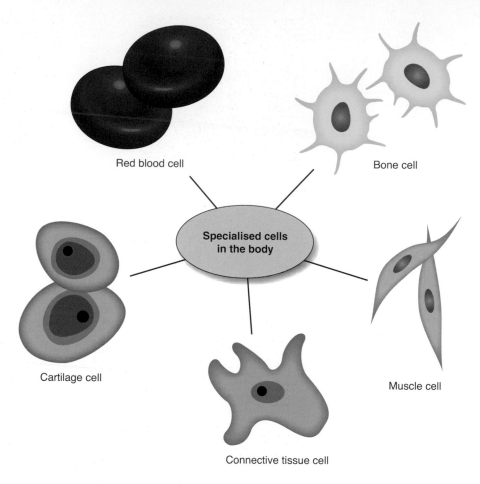

Red blood cell

Bone cell

Specialised cells in the body

Cartilage cell

Connective tissue cell

Muscle cell

Specialised cells in the human body

Activity 1

In small groups, research a specialised cell and label it. Describe underneath your diagram the function of each cell.

Groups of cells work together in large numbers to perform specialised functions and are called **tissues**. There are four main tissue types found in our body, with special functions:

- **Epithelial** – epithelial tissue is arranged in a single or multilayered sheet and usually covers internal and external surfaces of the body.
- **Connective** – blood, cartilage, bone, areolar, adipose. Connective tissue is supporting, it has fibres in it which are tough and non-elastic, e.g. cartilage, tendons, eyeball.

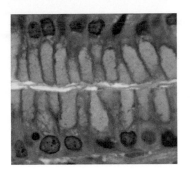

Epithelial tissue

Connective tissue

● **Muscle** – found in all muscles and special muscles like the heart.
● **Nervous** – consists of neurons to form the nervous system.

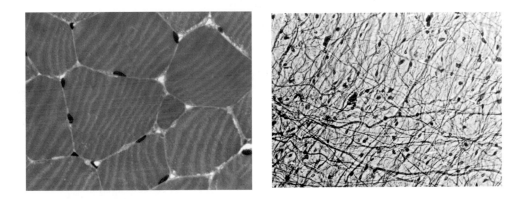

Muscle tissue

Nervous tissue

Several tissues can be grouped together to form a structure which carries out a particular function in the body: this is called an **organ.** For example, the stomach is an organ and contains epithelial tissue, muscle tissue and nervous tissue.

A group of organs which work together and whose functions are closely related is called a **system**. For example, the cardiovascular system is made up of blood vessels, blood and the heart. The nervous system is made up of the brain, the spinal cord and the nerves. These systems will be discussed later in this unit. To recap, examples of how a system is made are as follows:

CELL ⟶ TISSUE ⟶ ORGAN ⟶ SYSTEM

MUSCLE ⟶ **MUSCLE** ⟶ **HEART** ⟶ **CARDIOVASCULAR**
CELL   **TISSUE**   **SYSTEM**

Activity 2

As a class, divide into small groups, each taking one of the following organs:

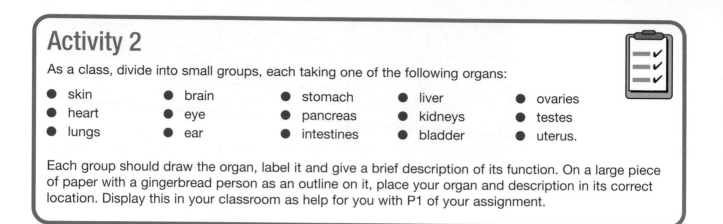

- skin
- heart
- lungs
- brain
- eye
- ear
- stomach
- pancreas
- intestines
- liver
- kidneys
- bladder
- ovaries
- testes
- uterus.

Each group should draw the organ, label it and give a brief description of its function. On a large piece of paper with a gingerbread person as an outline on it, place your organ and description in its correct location. Display this in your classroom as help for you with P1 of your assignment.

The following web links will give help with the structure and functions of human body organs: http://www.bupa.co.uk/health_information/asp/organ/ or use www.bbc.co.uk/science/humanbody and follow the interactive body link to play the organs game.

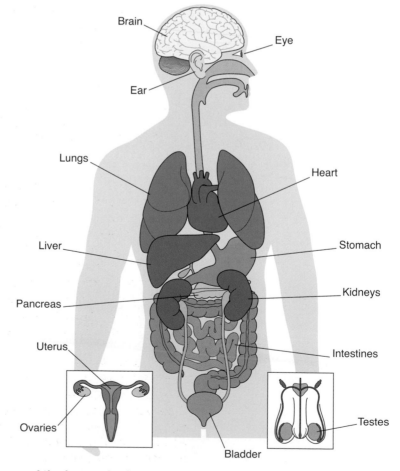

The organs of the human body

Organ	Main function	System
Skin	Protects the body from harmful bacteria with a waterproof barrier. It controls body temperature and has the ability to repair itself.	Excretory
Heart	A specialised muscle that contracts regularly and continuously, pumping blood to the body and the lungs. The pumping action is caused by a flow of electricity through the heart that repeats itself in a cycle.	Cardiovascular
Lungs	We have two lungs which supply our bodies with the vital oxygen required for our bodies to function properly. They are also responsible for getting rid of the waste product carbon dioxide.	Respiratory
Brain	The main control centre for the body which is responsible for all functions within the body, whether under voluntary or involuntary control.	Nervous
Eyes	Our eyes are moved by muscles, which allow us to look up and down and from side to side without moving our head. Normally both eyes work together to form a picture on the retina, which is then interpreted by the brain.	Nervous
Ears	The organs of hearing and balance. Our ears have three sections: outer ear, middle ear and inner ear. Noise or sound waves enter our outer ear and are channelled down the canal until they reach our eardrum. Once the sound wave reaches our eardrum, it vibrates and the sound waves then pass into the middle ear. Our middle ear is an air-filled cavity that links the outer ear with the inner ear.	Nervous
Stomach	A food bag that stores, warms and softens food and drink. It is able to expand and contract in response to how much it contains. It converts solids into fluid to promote digestion, squeezes food towards its exit and then squirts it rhythmically into the next part of the intestine.	Digestive

Organ	Main function	System
Pancreas	Produces digestive juices (enzymes) that continue the process of breaking down foods which begins in the stomach. The pancreas also produces hormones and insulin, which controls the balance of glucose between the blood and the rest of the body.	Digestive
Intestines	In the small intestine the food mixes with vital enzymes secreted by the liver and the pancreas. Fats and proteins are mainly digested in the small intestine. The large intestine receives the end products of the digestion process where water and other nutrients are absorbed. Waste products to be excreted are stored in the end segment known as the rectum.	Digestive
Liver	The centre of your metabolism. Complex chemical processes take place in the liver and it controls the body's absorption of food. It carries out more than 500 separate processes concerned with regulating all the main chemicals in blood and many other life-supporting functions.	Digestive
Kidneys	Filter the blood, clean it and keep its composition balanced. They maintain appropriate levels of fluids, minerals and other substances, including salt and water. They react to hormones from the brain and produce vital hormones of their own.	Excretory
Bladder	Urine drains from the kidneys into the bladder via two tubes – ureters. It is then stored in the bladder. The bladder stretches and fills and at a convenient time is emptied via another tube (urethra).	Excretory
Ovaries	There are two ovaries, one at each end of the fallopian tubes. The ovaries are responsible for the storage and release of eggs (ova). They produce the female hormones oestrogen and progesterone.	Reproductive
Testes	Men have two testes which are responsible for the production, storage and release of sperm. They produce the male hormone testosterone.	Reproductive
Uterus	Also known as the womb, it is a hollow, pear-shaped organ which has a thick blood supply and allows the implantation of the developing foetus and growth of the newborn.	Reproductive

2 Understand the structure, function and interrelationship of major body systems

Systems and their functions in the body

Cardiovascular system

The main function of the cardiovascular system is to transport oxygen and nutrients to the tissues and take away from the tissues carbon dioxide and other waste products. The cardiovascular system consists of:

● the heart
● the blood
● the blood vessels.

The heart

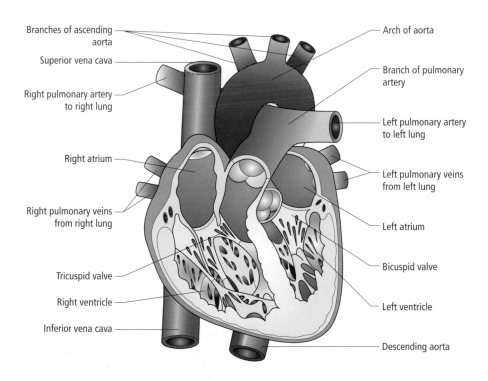

Branches of ascending aorta
Superior vena cava
Right pulmonary artery to right lung
Right atrium
Right pulmonary veins from right lung
Tricuspid valve
Right ventricle
Inferior vena cava

Arch of aorta
Branch of pulmonary artery
Left pulmonary artery to left lung
Left pulmonary veins from left lung
Left atrium
Bicuspid valve
Left ventricle
Descending aorta

The structure of the heart

The heart is a large muscle which contracts rhythmically so that the blood can be transported to the lungs to collect oxygen, then to the body, organs and tissues to deliver the oxygen. It then collects carbon dioxide from the body organs and tissues, taking it back to the heart and lungs. The heart is split into four chambers: two upper chambers (atria) and two lower chambers (ventricles).

The right side of the heart pumps the blood to the lungs to collect oxygen while the left side pumps blood around the body. The heart can be called a double pump. The left side of the heart muscle is much larger and thicker as it has a greater distance to pump the blood around.

Activity 3

Click onto the website below and follow the pathway of the blood through the heart with moving pictures and diagrams.
http://biologyinmotion.com/cardio/index.html

Oxygen-rich blood is carried in arteries to all tissues in the body, then blood with carbon dioxide from the tissues is taken back to the heart in veins. However, there is one exception to this rule.

Activity 4

Which artery carries deoxygenated blood? Which vein carries oxygenated blood? Why?

There are three types of blood vessels in our bodies:

1 Arteries.
2 Veins.
3 Capillaries.

The table below shows the differences between arteries and veins.

Arteries	Veins
Carry blood away from the heart	Carry blood towards the heart
Carry oxygenated blood	Carry deoxygenated blood
Blood flows rapidly	Blood flows slowly
Blood flows under high pressure	Blood flows under low pressure
Blood flows in pulses	Blood flows by squeezing action
Walls are thick	Walls are thin
Valves absent	Valves present
Internal diameter small	Internal diameter large
Cross-section round	Cross-section oval

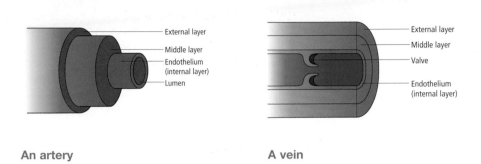

An artery　　　　　　　　　　**A vein**

Capillaries

Capillaries are thin-walled vessels which consist of a single layer of cells which allows oxygen, vitamins, minerals and water to be exchanged into the tissues to nourish the cells. Carbon dioxide and water then pass out of the cells to be excreted.

A capillary

Respiratory system

The function of the respiratory system is to deliver oxygen into the body by breathing in and to remove waste carbon dioxide from the body by breathing out. These actions are called **inspiration** (breathing in) and **expiration** (breathing out). The respiratory system consists of:

- mouth
- nose
- larynx (voice box)
- trachea
- lungs (x2)
- bronchus (x2)
- bronchioles
- alveoli.

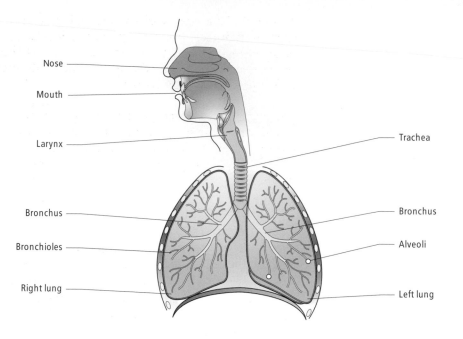

The respiratory system

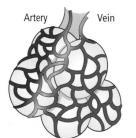

Alveoli

The respiratory system has a similar structure to the trunk and branches of a tree. Oxygen is breathed into the body and carbon dioxide is breathed out of the body via the trachea and bronchus. These are similar to the main trunk of the tree. The exchange of oxygen and carbon dioxide takes place at the end of the branches (bronchioles) in alveoli. The alveoli are structures like bunches of grapes which allow maximum crossover of gases back and forth to make the process efficient.

Activity 5

Put your hands on your ribcage and feel your breathing. Can you explain what happens when you breathe in and then breathe out?

The nervous system

The main functions of the nervous system are:

● to *receive* information from our external and internal environment
● to *interpret* (make sense of) this information
● and then to *take actions* accordingly.

This could be actions like walking, talking or running away. Or it could be actions such as reducing body temperature, increasing heart beat or regulating water balance. In this way, your nervous system is similar to a telephone exchange: it receives messages from all over the body, interprets them and sends out messages with answers to make changes.

The nervous system is split into two parts: the central nervous system – brain and spinal cord – and the peripheral nervous system – nerves. All messages are sent from sensory receptors via a sensory nerve to the brain or spinal cord. The brain or spinal cord then interprets the message and responses are made by the motor neurones to the effectors to make the change or movement.

The brain

The brain consists of billions of nerve cells. It is responding all the time to external and internal messages – those outside you and within you. For example, as you are reading this book your brain is interpreting information and allowing you to understand new ideas and perhaps make pictures. It will also be responding to external things, for instance are you feeling hot or cold? Your brain adjusts the internal environment to help you to feel comfortable, as well as creating feelings or emotions.

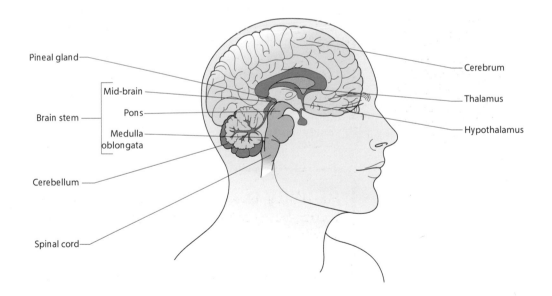

The brain

Spinal cord

This runs from the base of the brain to the lower part of the back (lumbar region). The spine is made up of 31 pairs of nerves which branch off to supply the body.

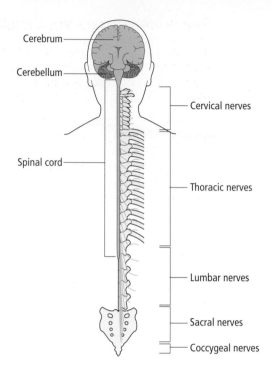

The spinal cord

Nerves

Nerves are made up of nerve cells or neurones and there are three basic kinds:

1 Sensory neurones.
2 Motor neurones.
3 Relay neurones.

Activity 6

Investigate the three types of neurones above. Write a brief summary of their functions and jobs and try to compare how they are different.

Activity 7

In small groups, draw up a table with two columns listing **voluntary** actions and **reflex** actions. Compare your findings. Which group has the most answers?

- **Reflex actions** – these are movements which you do without thinking, such as blinking or your mouth watering. These actions are done in response to external stimuli, but you do not always have control over them. Have you ever tried not blinking for a few minutes?
- **Voluntary actions** – these are actions which we do have control over. You can decide to walk, run, sit down, read or write. These actions are under your control.

The autonomic nervous system

This part of the nervous system is not under our control. It has two parts, called the sympathetic and parasympathetic nervous systems, which together are responsible for maintaining vital organs and the stability of the body internally (homeostasis). This is discussed later in the unit.

The endocrine system

The endocrine system produces chemical messages called **hormones**. These hormones are released by glands into the bloodstream. Once in the bloodstream, they target organs and can affect the structure and function of that part of the body. There are 39 hormones which work with the nervous system to maintain homeostasis in the body.

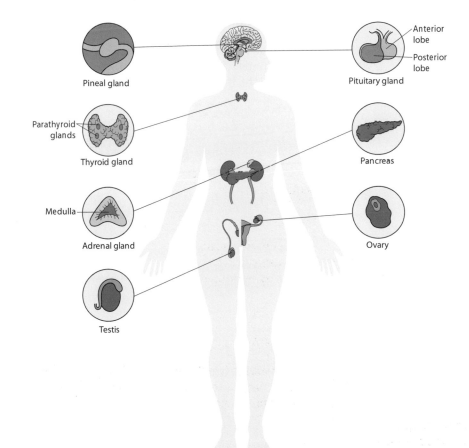

The endocrine system

The glands which secrete these hormones work in a system called negative feedback. Negative feedback means the gland is stimulated to produce more of the hormone when needed and to stop producing it when there is enough of the hormone in the body.

Activity 8

In pairs, choose any endocrine gland which is named on the diagram. Do some research into this gland and prepare a PowerPoint presentation for the class. You should try to include the following:

1 Name of the gland.
2 Where in the body it is situated.
3 Name of the hormones it secretes.
4 What the gland and hormones are responsible for.
5 Picture of what it looks like.

The digestive system

The digestive system or alimentary canal runs from your mouth to your anus and is approximately 8 metres long. Look at the picture below and see how many other organs in the body are involved in this system.

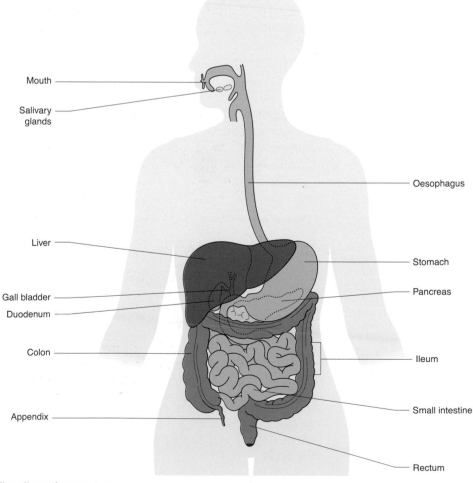

Mouth
Salivary glands
Oesophagus
Liver
Stomach
Gall bladder
Pancreas
Duodenum
Colon
Ileum
Appendix
Small intestine
Rectum

The digestive system

The digestive system consists of the mouth, salivary glands, pharynx, oesophagus, stomach, duodenum, ileum, colon, liver and pancreas.

Digestion takes place in two ways:

- physically – by your teeth and tongue, then the muscles in your alimentary canal break down the food into smaller pieces so that it is able to move through the gut
- chemically – enzymes and chemicals made by the digestive system are also responsible for breaking down the food.

Physical and chemical digestion take place at the same time – while the teeth and tongue are grinding and mashing the food, the enzymes can mix with the food to break it down even more.

Follow the web link below to watch the digestive system in action, then click on the link: How it works. http://www.constipationadvice.co.uk.

The process of digestion is as follows:

1. Ingestion – food is taken into the mouth and digestion starts.
2. Digestion – lumps of food are broken down physically and chemically.
3. Absorption – digested food passes through the gut wall and enters the bloodstream.
4. Assimilation – food is removed from the blood and used in the cells.
5. Egestion – undigested waste is removed from the body.

Activity 9

Study these five digestive processes in more detail. As a class, discuss where each one takes place within the digestive system. You could label a digestive tract with the numbers explaining why this is the correct area for that part of the digestion process.

The excretory system

This is also known as the renal system. It is the filter system in the body which eliminates waste products from the blood.

The main waste substances are:

- carbon dioxide – from all respiration
- water – from cell respiration and digestion
- urea – this is from the liver after it has broken down amino acids
- mineral salts – for example, sodium chloride.

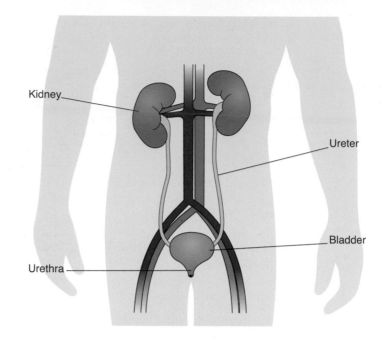

The renal system

The kidneys

You have two kidneys which filter the blood like a sieve. The kidneys keep in substances which are useful to the body and excrete waste substances together with water, which is called **urine**. Your kidneys also adjust the water, salt and acid balance of your blood through a process called **osmoregulation**.

The inside of a kidney has three regions:

1　Cortex.
2　Medulla.
3　Pelvis.

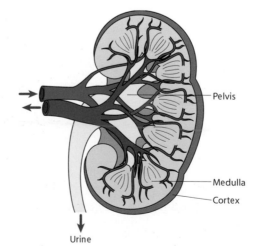

The structure of a kidney

Activity 10

In babies and young children the bladder is not under voluntary control, so nappies are very useful! At what age is the young child normally able to control their own bladder? How do they learn to control their bladder?

The ureters

These lead from the kidneys and take urine to the bladder. They are muscular tubes.

The bladder

This is the muscular storage sack for urine and when full (adult) can hold up to 500 ml. Emptying the bladder, or urination, is under voluntary control in most adults. This is triggered by the sensory nerves in the bladder which send messages to the brain that the bladder is ready to be emptied.

The urethra

This is the muscular tube which runs from the bladder to the outside of the body. In women the urethra is about 4cm long and in men it is about 20cm long as it runs through the penis.

Reproductive systems

This system is involved in the production of specialised cells called sex cells or gametes (eggs and sperm). It is in these gametes that the characteristics of each parent can be found and are transferred to the newborn baby. When an egg and sperm join together it is called fertilisation and the combined cells are known as a zygote. It now contains characteristics (genes) from both parents.

The male reproductive system has three main functions:

1   The testes produce sperm.
2   The penis deposits sperm inside the female reproductive system.
3   The testes produce the hormone testosterone (you will have investigated this in the endocrine system).

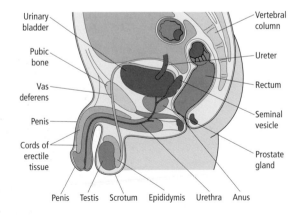

The male reproductive system

The female reproductive system has four main functions:

1   The ovaries produce eggs or ova.
2   The uterus provides a safe environment for the developing foetus where it can be nourished.

3   The ovaries produce the hormones oestrogen and progesterone (you will have investigated these in the endocrine system).
4   The mammary glands (breasts) produce milk for the newborn baby.

Activity 11

Get into small groups to investigate the reproductive system. If possible, present the main information in a flowchart presentation which will highlight the function of the reproductive system. The main reproductive processes you will need to explain are:

● sperm production
● fertilisation
● ovulation
● ejaculation
● the menstrual cycle.

The musculoskeletal system

This system contains the muscles and bones of the body. Its function is to provide support and movement of the body as well as protection of vital body organs.

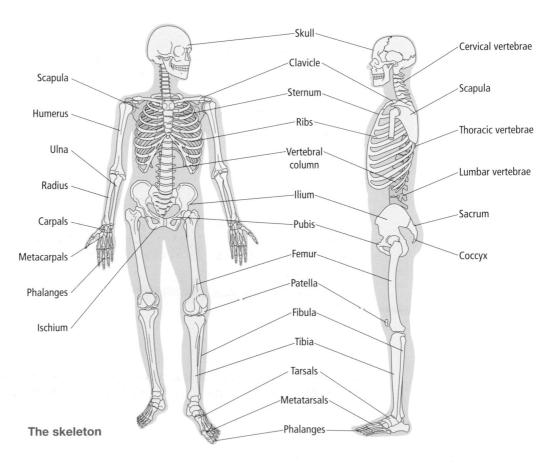

The skeleton

The skeleton

This is made up of 206 separate bones and has the following functions:

- Provides movements and something for muscles to attach to.
- Protects vital organs such as brain, heart and lungs.
- Some bones produce new blood cells.
- Assists with blood clotting as it produces calcium.

The skeleton is divided into two separate parts:

1 The axial skeleton – skull, ribcage and backbone.
2 The appendicular skeleton – pectoral girdle and the pelvic girdle, the arms and the legs.

Activity 12

Divide into two large groups. Each take a part of the skeleton and research what the bones are called in your section. Print a picture of the skeleton from a website and label it. (See, for example, http://upload.wikimedia.org/wikipedia/commons/thumb/8/85/Human_skeleton_front.svg/270px-Human_skeleton_front.svg.png.)

Joints

Where the ends of two bones meet is called a joint. There are over 200 places where this happens in your body. There are 3 types of joints:

1 Moveable joints, e.g. shoulder, elbow, knee.
2 Slightly moveable joints, e.g. spine.
3 Immoveable joints, e.g. skull.

Activity 13

Joints can also be classed according to how they move. Investigate the following types of joints and explain their movement, giving an example within the body:
- hinge joint
- ball and socket joint
- sliding joint.

Bones are held together with **ligaments**. These are pieces of strong connective tissue. Ligaments contract and extend, in order to allow movement of the bones.

Activity 14

- Why do children need to drink milk?
- What is rickets?
- What is osteoporosis?

Muscles

Muscle makes up a large percentage of our body weight and can be split into three different types:

1. Striped, skeletal muscle or voluntary muscles – these are attached to the bones and appear striped under a microscope. They are responsible for movement. They can tire easily. We have to tell this muscle what to do.
2. Involuntary or smooth muscles – these are found inside organs like the digestive organs, blood vessels and urethras. They are responsible for contracting and relaxing and moving food, blood and urine through them. They work constantly and never tire.
3. Cardiac muscle – this is found only in the heart and contracts at least 70 times a minute constantly.

Activity 15

Look at the pictures below and explain how muscles move bones. Use the following KidsHealth web link to help you: http://www.kidshealth.org/parent/general/body_basics/ bones_muscles_joints.html.

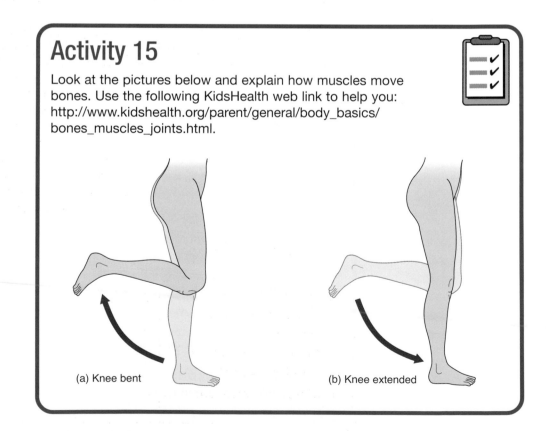

(a) Knee bent   (b) Knee extended

To help you with P2 and M1 in your assignment, choose two of the above systems you have just read about and explain their:

- structure (what organs the system is made up of)
- function (how the system works).

Interrelationship

Although the systems you have just read about all work to provide a main function for the body, it is clear that their job cannot be done without the help of other body systems. Therefore systems within the body rely on each other to maintain correct body functioning. For example, the cardiovascular system relies on the respiratory system to provide oxygen from the lungs to give to the heart to pump around the body. The cardiovascular system then returns deoxygenated blood to the heart, then the lungs, to drop off the carbon dioxide and pick up new supplies of oxygen.

Activity 16

This will help you with D1 in your assignment.
In the table below are suggestions of other systems which work together in the body. Copy and fill in the last column with their functions (the first one has been done for you). Write your findings in a flowchart format to help you before you explain their function.

Body systems	How they work together
Cardiovascular system and respiratory system	The respiratory system delivers oxygen to the blood from the lungs. It is taken to the heart in the cardiovascular system which pumps blood around the body via blood vessels. Carbon dioxide is picked up in the blood and is taken back to the heart in blood vessels where the heart pumps the blood back to the lungs for new oxygen supplies.
Nervous system and musculoskeletal system	
Digestive system and cardiovascular system	
Reproductive system and endocrine system	
Excretory system and endocrine system	
Digestive system and endocrine system	

Homeostasis

Homeostasis is the mechanism in our bodies which regulates and maintains a stable and constant internal environment. To help us understand homeostasis, imagine your body is similar to your home and your homeostatic mechanism is your central heating system. Within the system is a thermostat which regulates the heating system, similar to the hypothalamus in our brain, which regulates our internal environment. The hypothalamus is the control centre.

Our bodies are continuously making adjustments to regulate normal body functions. Fortunately these adjustments are done automatically, otherwise we would be very busy people, regulating our internal environment frequently.

Homeostasis is described as a **negative feedback system**. This simply means that the system is able to take corrective action to maintain a constant environment. This can be further explained in the diagram below.

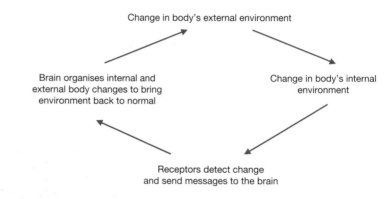

Homeostasis: a negative feedback system

Homeostasis is responsible for maintaining the constant level of many body functions, e.g.:

- body temperature
- blood pressure
- breathing rate/oxygen supply
- blood glucose levels.

Body temperature

Homeostasis cannot take place without detectors and correctors. Look at the diagram opposite and corrective action the body takes to maintain a constant body temperature.

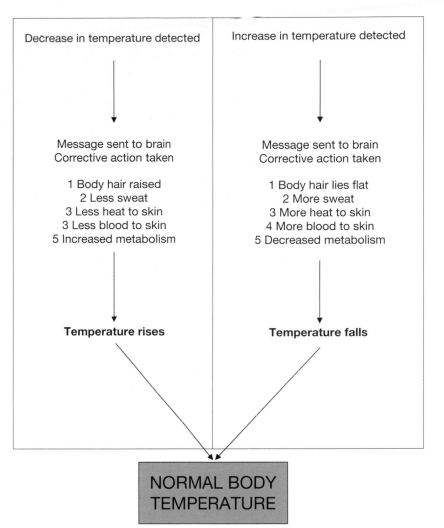

Decrease in temperature detected	Increase in temperature detected
↓	↓
Message sent to brain Corrective action taken	Message sent to brain Corrective action taken
1 Body hair raised 2 Less sweat 3 Less heat to skin 3 Less blood to skin 5 Increased metabolism	1 Body hair lies flat 2 More sweat 3 More heat to skin 4 More blood to skin 5 Decreased metabolism
↓	↓
Temperature rises	**Temperature falls**

NORMAL BODY TEMPERATURE

There are also behavioural actions that we take in response to a rise or fall in body temperature, e.g.:

● have warm or cold drinks
● put on or take off clothing
● take exercise
● switch on a fan.

Blood pressure

The heart rate and blood pressure are under the control of the autonomic nervous system and also are affected by hormones so are under the control of the endocrine system. The system also follows the principles of the negative feedback system. We do not tell our heart rate to increase or slow down.

What makes our heart rate change?

1 Exercise.
2 Fear.
3 Excitement.

The cardiovascular centre in the brain controls the heartbeat, which affects the blood pressure. If the heart rate needs to increase, messages are sent along the sympathetic nervous system and the heart rate increases. If the heart rate then needs to slow down, messages are sent along the parasympathetic nervous system and the heart rate decreases. The detectors which send these messages back and forth are chemical receptors in the heart, blood vessels and brain. These detectors constantly monitor the blood and the level of carbon dioxide and oxygen. When necessary, adjustments are made to correct to the normal rate – arteries widen to lower the blood pressure or narrow to increase the blood pressure.

Breathing rate

Respiration or breathing rate is controlled by nerve impulses from the respiratory centre in the brain. It controls:

- the rhythm of breathing
- the depth of breathing
- the rate of breathing.

This centre also follows the principle of negative feedback and stimulates a change in respirations when receptors in the blood sense a decrease or increase in the amount of circulating carbon dioxide. For example, during exercise when the receptors detect a high level of carbon dioxide in the bloodstream, they send messages to the brain to increase and deepen the breathing rate in order to expel carbon dioxide and replenish oxygen.

Our breathing rate is also under voluntary control – we can alter our rate of breathing or hold our breath if we wish!

Blood glucose level

The control of blood sugar level in the blood follows the same principle – the negative feedback loop. The control centre here is in the pancreas where receptors monitor the concentration of glucose in the bloodstream and hormones control the correct balance. The hormones are responsible for the control of:

1 Insulin – which lowers blood sugar levels.
2 Glucagon – which raises blood sugar levels.

Study the table below to understand the body response after a meal (i.e. high blood sugar level) and when hungry (i.e. low blood sugar level).

Eating	Hungry
Carbohydrates in food digested and changed to glucose	Low blood sugar level
Glucose high in blood	Pancreas produces the hormone glucagon
Pancreas produces insulin	Changes glycogen from the liver into glucose so it can be used in the body
Some glucose stored in liver as glycogen, some used by cells	Blood glucose level rises to normal
Blood sugar level decreases to normal	Pancreas stops producing glucagon

3 Investigate how monitoring body systems through routine measurements and observations can indicate malfunctions

As a professional in a health and social care setting it may be necessary for you to measure and record how the main body systems are functioning. To do this you need to know the following:

1   How to measure the system accurately.
2   What equipment to use and how to use it safely.
3   What the normal measurements are for that system.
4   How to record the measurement accurately.

It is important to establish what is called a **baseline set of observations** to give to the doctors or supervisors in the care setting. This gives information to professionals to be able to treat and diagnose service users and to follow improvement or decline of their condition. The observations will then be taken at regular intervals to show a pattern of measurements. We must remember that not all service users are the same. Many factors will alter readings and these have to be taken into account when taking observations from service users.

Routine physiological measurements

Pulse rate

The pulse is the rhythmical beat from the heart as the arteries expand and contract. It gives an idea of how well the cardiovascular system is working. A pulse can be felt anywhere in the body where an artery travels over a bone. The most common places for feeling a pulse are wrist-radial pulse and neck-carotid pulse.

The pulse is recorded in beats per minute (bpm). When taking a pulse rate, the beats should always be counted for a full minute.

Activity 17

Discuss the factors in the diagram. Would they increase or decrease the pulse rate?

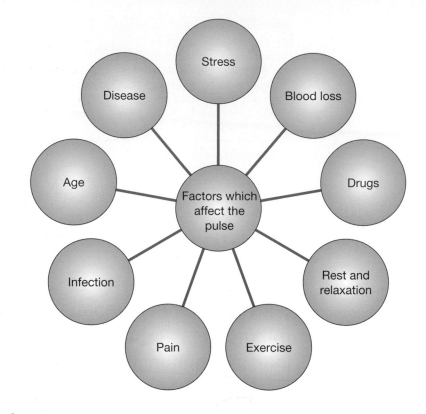

Blood pressure

Blood pressure is the force exerted by the blood on the vessel walls. Again this is a measurement to monitor the cardiovascular system. Blood pressure can vary over the body depending on where the pressure is taken. It is usually measured in the arm with a machine and an inflatable cuff. Nowadays these are very often battery operated (older styles tend to be manually operated).

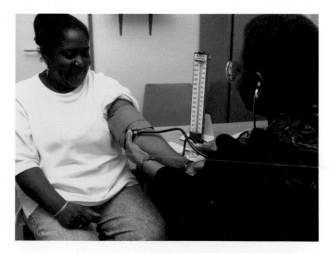

A person having their blood pressure measured

Activity 18

From the diagram below, pick out the lifestyle factors which may affect blood pressure.
Discuss how they can be altered.

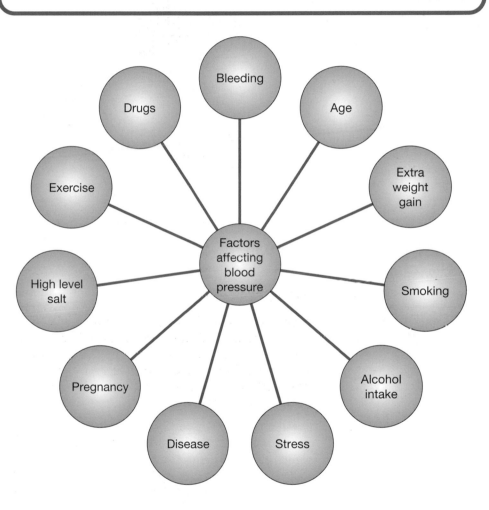

Breathing rate

Breathing is the process by which the body gains oxygen and gets rid of carbon dioxide. Breathing rate is measured by watching the movement of the chest – one breath in (inspiration) and one breath out (expiration) are counted as one respiration. When measuring breathing rate, it should be counted for a full minute. Occasionally respirations may be shallow, so it may be necessary (with permission) to rest your hand lightly on the person's chest.

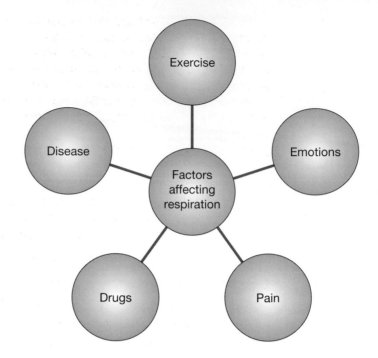

Peak flow

Peak flow monitors the respiratory system. A peak flow meter is a small device that you blow into and is used commonly with asthmatic service users. It measures the fastest rate of air (airflow) that you can blow out of your lungs. It records airflow in litres per minute (l/min). A single reading is not very useful in helping decide how well the lungs are functioning – it is advisable to take three readings of peak flow and record the highest.

Body temperature

The temperature of the body needs to be kept fairly stable as dramatic changes can seriously affect the body's systems. Body temperature monitors how effectively the homeostatic mechanisms are controlled in your body. Temperature is measured in °C.

There are different ways to measure a temperature as well as different places on the body where temperature can be taken:

● tympanic thermometers – in the ear
● liquid crystal display (LCD) strip thermometers – on the forehead
● digital thermometers – in the mouth or under the arm (for young children and babies you are advised not to put a thermometer in their mouth).

Blood glucose levels

Blood glucose (sugar) readings are usually done for those service users who have diabetes. Blood sugar levels monitor how effective the pancreas is at producing and using the hormone insulin. The blood sugar level is the amount of glucose (sugar) in the blood, expressed as (mmol/l).

To check blood sugar level, put a small amount of blood on a test strip. Now place the strip into the glucose meter. After about 30 seconds it will display the blood glucose level. The best way to take a blood sample is by pricking your finger with a sharp lancet that is designed to penetrate the skin only as far as needed to draw a drop of blood. However, new devices have been produced which avoid the need to pierce the skin. These are called **non-invasive** methods. See, for example, http://staffnurse.com/nursing-news-articles/non-invasive-blood-glucose-test-1668.html.

Activity 19

Get into small groups and look into the following procedures. Find out all the important points and prepare an information leaflet for a care worker. Make sure you give them clear instructions about how to measure the following:

pulse rate   breathing rate   temperature

blood pressure   peak flow   blood glucose level.

Include the following information and draw up clear diagrams:
● how to position the service user
● how to take and record the above measurements
● what the normal range is for an adult
● what equipment you may need.

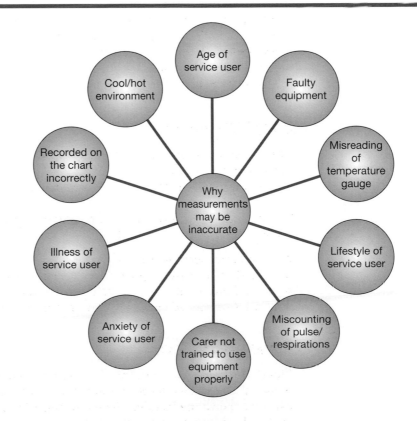

Reasons why measurements may be inaccurate

Legislation and regulations

In your work setting, the **Health and Safety at Work Act 1974** provides the main guidelines for health and safety in the workplace. It is called an umbrella for other regulations.

Activity 20

Investigate the regulations under the Health and Safety at Work Act. Find out which parts are relevant to your work setting.

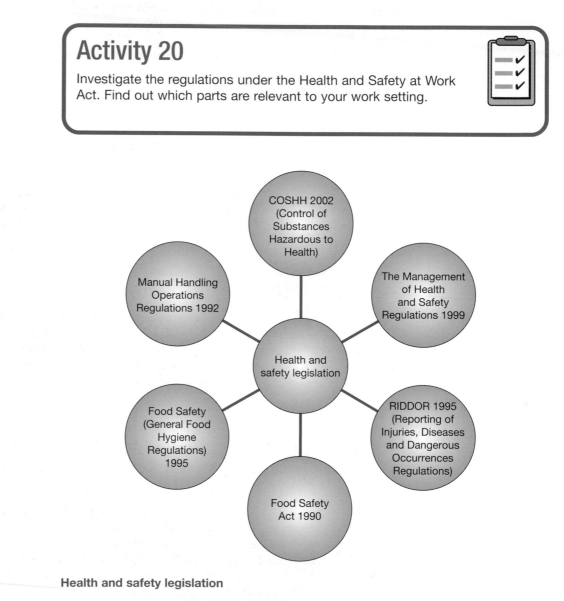

Health and safety legislation

Other observations

When taking vital readings from the service user it is important that we look at other physical signs the service user may be showing. If necessary, we should report these to our supervisors.

Look at the diagram below and discuss what signs a care worker should look for. Discuss what possible reasons could be causing these.

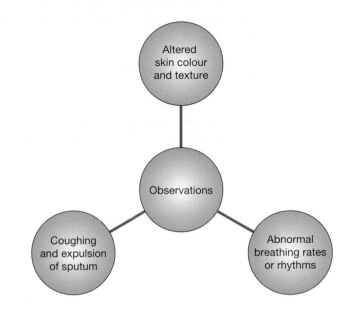

Help towards P3, M2 and D2

In your Unit 5 assignment you need to consider the two systems you have just written about in P2 and describe what routine measurements are used to monitor these systems. Then explain the normal ranges of these measurements and what malfunctions are occurring if the readings are above or below normal. You should also explain how these measurements can be used to help identify health and illhealth.

4 Examine malfunctions in body systems and resultant needs of patients/service users

A malfunction is a partial or total failure of a system to work correctly. As discussed in the previous section, one of the reasons for measuring and observing bodily systems is to detect any abnormality or malfunction in that system. In this section we will research malfunctions of the major body systems and what factors may lead to them. We will also look at how to care for those individuals who may suffer the effects of certain conditions.

Activity 21

Towards P4, P5, P6 and M3.

In the spider diagram below, there are some conditions which you may have come across when caring for individuals in your care settings. In pairs, choose one condition and prepare an information leaflet for the individual's relatives. You should include the following information:

● name of the condition
● signs and symptoms of the condition
● what risk factors may be associated with the condition
● what care needs may be involved in looking after a person with this particular condition.

Some of these websites may be helpful when collecting information for this task:

http://www.bupa.co.uk/health_information/asp/your_health/factsheets
http://www.bbc.co.uk/health
http://www.netdoctor.co.uk/diseases.

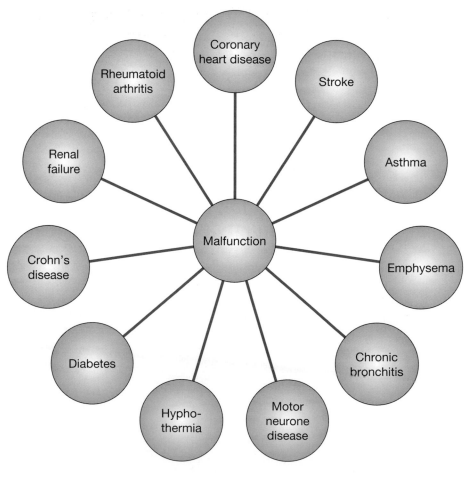

Different types of conditions

As a care worker, it is important that you **always** treat individual service users with dignity and respect. Remember, you are not just treating the symptoms of a disease, you are caring for an individual's **holistic** needs. In other words, all the parts of an individual are important, not just one part.

SUMMARY

After working through this unit you should be able to:

- identify the position and main function of the main organs of the human body

- describe the structure and function of two of the major body systems

- describe the routine measurements and observations used to monitor two body systems

- identify a malfunction in two major body systems

- identify risk factors for each of these two malfunctions

- describe the care that should be given to service users with these two malfunctions.

Grading grid

In order to pass this unit, the evidence that the learner presents for assessment needs to demonstrate that they can meet all of the learning outcomes for the unit. The criteria for a pass grade describe the level of achievement required to pass this unit.

Grading criteria

To achieve a pass grade the evidence must show that the learner is able to:	To achieve a merit grade the evidence must show that, in addition to the pass criteria, the learner is able to:	To achieve a distinction grade the evidence must show that, in addition to the pass and merit criteria, the learner is able to:
P1 identify the position and functions of the main organs of the human body	**M1** explain the structure of two body systems in relation to their functions	**D1** explain how two systems of the body interrelate to perform a named function
P2 describe the structure and function of two of the major body systems	**M2** explain how measurements and observations taken on these body systems could indicate malfunction	**D2** explain how routine measurements and observations can be used as indicators of health/ill health
P3 describe the routine measurements and observations used to monitor these two body systems	**M3** explain the link between the malfunction of the two body systems and the care the patients/service users receive	
P4 identify a malfunction in each of the two major body systems described		
P5 identify risk factors for each of the two malfunctions		
P6 describe the care that should be given to patients/service users with these two malfunctions		

Human Lifespan Development

This unit provides knowledge and understanding of development through all the life stages. It looks at how to assist with individual needs at different stages of life. It also promotes an understanding of different life events and their positive and negative influences during the life stages. We will look at social and economic factors, and self-concept, and how these factors impact upon development.

Learning Outcomes

On completion of this unit you should be able to:

1 Investigate the developmental changes that occur at different life stages
2 Explore positive and negative influences on individuals at different life stages
3 Examine the factors that can influence an individual's self-concept
4 Investigate changing care needs at different life stages.

1 Investigate the developmental changes that occur at different life stages

All human beings start from the moment of conception – when a sperm meets and fertilises an egg – but not all human beings develop in the same way. Many factors influence the rate and type of growth and development. These are factors not just from our genetic make-up but from external influences around us. There is a pattern to human growth and development but we do not all follow the same pattern at the same rate.

KEY TERMS

Growth is an increase in physical size. Most babies grow bigger.

Development is an increase in skills. Babies learn to talk and to smile. Teenagers learn to use MP3 players. An older person may learn a new language before going on holiday abroad.

Growth is not the same as development. Some people grow but do not develop. Sometimes babies are born with brain damage and do not develop the skills of walking and talking. A pregnant woman who gets German measles may feel unwell. If she is in the early stages of pregnancy, the virus can cause severe damage to the unborn baby. For more on this, see the Medinfo website (www.medinfo.co.uk/conditions/rubella.html).

Activity 1

Human development can be divided into four different areas:
1 Physical.
2 Intellectual.
3 Emotional.
4 Social.

Below is a list of explanations. Can you match them to the development areas above?

A – Problem solving, language development, reading and writing skills, memory, concentration and creativity.
B – Getting on with others, how to behave in different situations, becoming part of a group and making friends.
C – Development of the body structure and its system, how the body works, how each part of the body relates to other parts.
D – Developing feelings towards each other, making sense of your own feelings, becoming aware of your identity and self-image.

ANSWERS: 1 – C, 2 – A, 3 – D, 4 – B.

Conception

A woman is usually fertile around two weeks after her menstrual period. An egg is released from the ovary and travels along the fallopian tube. If sexual intercourse takes place, it is in the fallopian tubes that fertilisation will take place by the male sperm. Millions of sperm are released by the man during ejaculation, although only one sperm is needed to fertilise a female egg.

When the egg and sperm meet, they start to divide and quickly become a ball of cells. Over a few days, this ball of cells travels into the uterus and attaches itself to the uterus wall, where it starts to develop into a new human being. This process of the egg and sperm joining and starting to divide is known as fertilization – 23 chromosomes from the sperm and 23 chromosomes from the egg join and provide the genetic make-up for a new human being.

Activity 2

Go to http://www.babycentre.co.uk/pregnancy – this website gives information and pictures from 4 to 40 weeks of pregnancy. In small groups, choose a stage of pregnancy and investigate what is happening to the baby and the mother. You may like to display your findings in a poster, highlighting each month's development.

Birth and infancy 0–3 years

A normal pregnancy is around 40 to 42 weeks long. As we noted earlier, our development can depend very much on internal and external factors. Pregnancy is the first important stage, when many factors can affect the growth of a baby.

Activity 3

Get into small groups within the class. Put some ideas together and suggest why growth and development can be affected by internal and external factors. Try to think of positive and negative factors. Here are some ideas to start with.

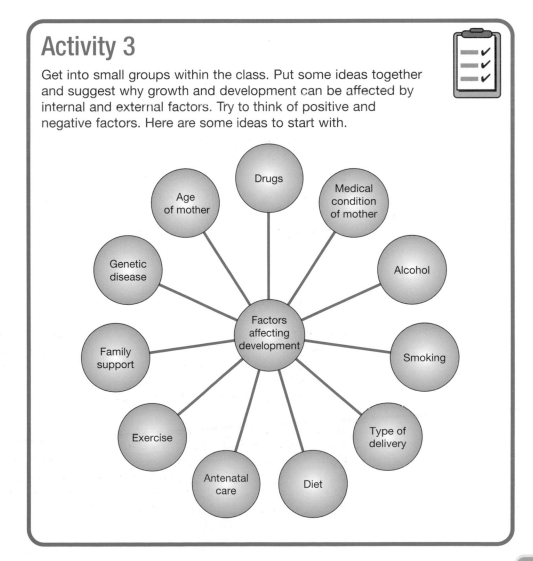

Physical development

At this development stage, physical development is rapid. The increase from newborn to three years old physically is tremendous. Physical development can be split into two categories:

● gross motor skills – large movements: kicking, hopping, skipping, jumping, running, walking.
● fine motor skills – small movements: threading, picking up small things, holding objects

Gross motor skills

When babies are born, they have little control over their head if it is not supported by an adult. By six months they usually have complete head control. By nine months they are generally able to pull themselves up to a sitting position, and then to stand alone by 12 months. By around 15 months most babies can walk alone and at two years old most can walk up and down stairs with two feet on one step. By three years old, most children can climb the stairs properly.

Do remember, babies and children may develop crawling and walking skills earlier or later than others. These development stages are just average guidelines for parents and professionals – it is perfectly normal for babies to develop at different rates.

Activity 4

Study the pictures. Put an age to each child and suggest which gross motor skills are being displayed.

Fine motor skills

Newborn babies keep their hands closed most of the time. They have an automatic grasp reflex, which usually disappears by about three months old. By six months a child will generally voluntarily grasp an object or toy and hold it. The movements in the hands become more refined by nine months and most children can use finger and thumb to hold objects. By 12 months they can usually hold a crayon using the 'palmar grasp'. At 15 months they can usually take a spoon to their mouth and by two years old they may begin to dress themselves.

Activity 5

Study the pictures and put an age to each child and suggest which fine motor skill they are displaying.

Intellectual development

This area of development is rapid and includes development of language. Think of a newborn and how they attract people's attention, then think of a three-year-old and how they attract people's attention. They have gone from crying to talking, often in full sentences. Intellectual development also includes using the senses.

Question: What are the five senses that we have?
Newborn babies use their senses to explore their surroundings. They are aware of bright colours and sounds. By six months old they are beginning to tell the difference between familiar sights and tastes. Have you noticed babies always put objects straight in their mouths? Why do you think this might be?

From six months onwards they repeat actions like dropping a toy from a pram, but they have only a short attention span. From 12 months onwards they are beginning to understand the world around them and have increased curiosity. By the age of two they can usually point to familiar parts of the body and do simple jigsaws. By the age of three they will generally start to understand the concepts of over, under and behind and they enjoy listening to stories.

Emotional development

Emotional development is encouraged and supported if the baby has a constant caregiver. This provides them with a firm feeling of stability and attachment. This sense of attachment is called **bonding**. Newborn infants may cry if they are left alone too long or not held firmly because they do not feel a sense of security.

As they reach three months old they can wriggle with pleasure and show happiness. At six months old they may show anxiety towards strangers and at 12 months old they can show emotions like anger – for example, if a toy is taken away from them. At two years old they may start to have tantrums – have you heard of the 'terrible twos'? However, at this age they are trying to become more independent. By three years of age they may copy the moods or behaviour of adults around them, so having positive role models is very important.

Activity 6

What is a role model? Did you have a role model when you were growing up?
Try to think of some things you could do to encourage a young child to have a positive, happy attitude. Now try to think of some negative attitudes or behaviours which might influence young children.

Social development

Between the age of birth and three months, babies will start to smile at familiar faces. By the age of six months they may well get upset when their mother leaves the room and may not be confident with others. At 12 months they enjoy being with familiar people and they usually enjoy mealtimes. At two years they often enjoy helping others and they may show concern for other children who may be upset. By three years old they will probably begin to take turns when playing with other children and are becoming more independent.

Activity 7

A stage of social development is learning to play between the ages of 1 to 5 years. Investigate the following stages of play:

- solitary play
- parallel play

Childhood 4–10 years

Physical development

In this life stage children's physical development is showing strength, agility and dexterity. The rate of growth is now steady.

Intellectual development

At the age of four, when a child's concentration span is much longer, children in this country usually begin their full-time compulsory education. By the age of five they may start to draw quite detailed pictures and even enjoy solving problems. Moving towards the age of ten, children will start thinking in a more complex way and be able to perform simple tasks whilst listening to instructions. Language development is also an important aspect: four-year-olds start to talk in full sentences – and they will be asking many questions!

By the age of five most children will be enjoying books and carrying out longer conversations with others. By ten years of age most children will be fluent talkers and show an understanding of others' points of view.

Another important part of intellectual development is moral development. This means that, as children grow up, they start to develop an understanding of the differences between right and wrong. Parents and carers are the main influence on children's moral development. Two important theorists, Piaget and Kohlberg, have discussed the development of 'moral thinking' and published their ideas about the links between intellectual development and morals.

Activity 10

Follow the web link below and make some brief notes on the thoughts of Jean Piaget and Lawrence Kohlberg.

- Do you feel that moral development is influenced by anything else?
- Role models in the media, friends and family can affect how children see what is right and wrong. What do you think?
- Should politicians, pop stars and TV personalities behave in a positive way?

http://www.open2.net/healthliving/family_childdevelopment/morality.html

Activity 11

In groups, choose one of the following age groups: 4, 5, 7, 10. Visit your local library (or college/school library) and suggest some books for a child of that age group. Explain why you have chosen them for your age group. Think about the words, sentences and pictures they contain. Are they appropriate for that age range? How will they encourage reading?
Can you remember which books helped you learn to read?

Emotional development

Emotional development is about developing the ability to understand and control one's emotions. As children grow up, they start to understand more about their feelings and the feelings of others. This is a gradual process throughout childhood – and it carries on for most of our lives!

Story time with an adult helps a child to develop reading skills

From the age of five children start to become more confident and want to do well at school and in games. While a six-year-old may show signs of frustration when they fail at something, by the age of eight they are becoming more emotionally stable. In this life stage children's behaviour may be difficult to handle at times because they are developing control over their emotions. There are also other important factors that can affect children's behaviour – see the diagram below.

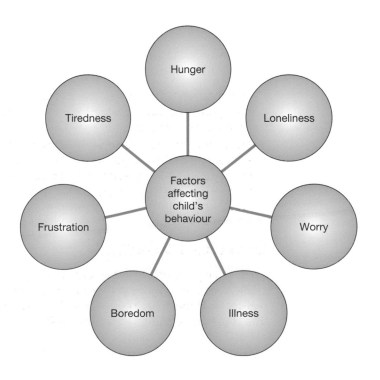

Social development

The four-year-old child still depends on their parents and carers to provide social activities for them and to help them with the new social skills they are learning. For example, they still need help with dressing, eating with a knife and fork and going to the toilet. As they grow, most five- and six-year-olds like to choose their own friends and decide on play activities. By the age of ten they will generally develop much fuller awareness of social skills and also be aware of rules and the need to co-operate with others.

Adolescence 11–18 years of age

This life stage is the change from childhood to adulthood.

Physical development

Physically during this life stage girls and boys start **puberty**. During puberty, physical changes prepare the body for sexual reproduction.

Female changes	Male changes
Breasts develop	Facial hair
Pubic hair grows	Pubic hair grows
Weight gain	Growth spurt
Growth spurt	Growth of penis and testes
Periods start	Voice deepens

These physical changes in appearance have a great effect on the other developmental areas of the adolescent.

Intellectual development

During this life stage the adolescent will study for formal examinations at school and they may choose to study further subjects at the age of 16. Their vocabulary increases and they are able to talk to people of all ages. They start to develop a sense of values and beliefs, and they may question the world around them. Adolescence can be a very impressionable age – adolescents often make lifestyle choices which have positive or negative effects on their future.

Emotional development

This stage of development for adolescents can be described as an emotional rollercoaster. They are coping with major physical changes to their bodies. Socially, they strive to be accepted by their peer groups. Emotionally and physically, they may be attracted to the same or the opposite sex and they are also faced with issues of self-esteem and self-concept (discussed later in this unit).

They may be studying for important examinations, leaving home, forming important emotional relationships, becoming independent and moving from education to the world of work. Think about your own adolescence. Would you agree it is an exhausting time?

Social development

This is a crucial stage for making relationships and fitting in with peer groups. It is a time to establish identity and explore sexuality. The adolescent may experience conflict with parents as they begin to form their own ideas about the world and how to be independent. They may be entering the world of professional employment as well as establishing relationships in other areas.

Adulthood 18–65 years old

It is difficult to say what marks adulthood as it can vary in different cultures. In this country we are able to vote at the age of 18 and also legally buy alcohol. However, you can legally marry at 16 with your parent's consent and join the Armed Forces. You can also finish compulsory education and go into employment at 16.

Activity 12

Has anyone ever said to you: *Let's talk about this like adults?*
Grow up, stop acting like a child!

When or what makes you an adult? Discuss this with your classmates.

The life stage of adulthood could be split into further categories:

● Young adulthood.
● Middle adulthood.
● Late adulthood.

Physical development

Young adulthood is often a time of high physical fitness in men and women. Women are most fertile at this time and many have their children in their twenties and thirties. High-risk pregnancies increase with the age of the mother. Women around the age of 45 to 55 years old reach the menopause.

As middle adulthood approaches some people notice a decline in sensory activity, for example they may need to wear glasses or may not be able to hear certain sounds or noise pitches. Hair loss in men is common. Adults at this life stage may be less active, so may suffer middle-age spread. They still eat the same amount of food, but they gain weight because of lower activity levels. In late adulthood there is an increased risk of health problems associated with age.

Intellectual development

In young adulthood, students complete their full-time education and may go on to study for other qualifications and specialist studies, at college or university. They usually have a good memory and long concentration span. By late adulthood, many complex intellectual and social skills are acquired, as well as plenty of life experience and wisdom to pass on to others.

Emotional development

During adulthood, most people's self-esteem and confidence increase, providing that emotional factors in their lives are positive and their personal relationships are stable.

Social development

New social relationships are made through the world of work. Many young adults meet their life partner through work. Later in adulthood, social relationships may be put under pressure as marriage and parenting play their part. It is possible that the family income may reduce when one parent cuts down their working hours or leaves work to bring up the children, making family life quite tiring or stressful. Later on, in middle adulthood, as children grow up, become more independent and leave home, parents may go back to work. Other activities may be resumed and previous freedoms and pleasures may return.

In later adulthood, as retirement approaches, older people may lose some social relationships from work or if their partner dies. However, for many people social activities increase as they have the extra time and money to enjoy their retirement.

Old age – 65 years onwards

Generally at the age of 65 most people retire from full-time work or reduce their employment commitments. However, owing to the fact that the population is living longer, people are now working longer. Also, because of healthier lifestyles and medical progress, a lot of older people can maintain good health. Therefore a 65-year-old may not see themselves as old. It can be a time of life to begin new challenges rather than for slowing down and taking life easy.

Activity 13

Split into four groups.

Each group should choose one development area:

- physical
- intellectual
- emotional
- social.

Activity 13 (continued)

In terms of old age, present a poster about your development area. Try to include the following things:

● physical ability
● physical changes
● physical malfunctions
● intellectual skills
● self-esteem
● self-concept
● social contacts
● family contacts
● relationships.

Look at your findings and discuss each area of development with the other groups. Highlight the changes, positive and negative. Try to think of an elderly person you know in this life stage to help you with your answers.

The final stage of life

The final stage of life is not always in old age (we could die at any age), but statistics show that more than 80 per cent of us will die after the age of 65. Death occurs when our bodies stop functioning biologically. This can be due to many causes. In previous centuries, people were much more familiar with death as it was all around them, in both the young and the old. Today developments in medical science have removed death from our everyday life. Instead of believing in the afterlife, these days many of us put our hope in finding a treatment or cure to prolong life.

Some people have very little experience of death in their families. In modern life, death is not usually talked about very much in this country. Some people fear death and therefore do not think about it or discuss it. They feel uncomfortable in the company of people who talk about death. Other people have open views about death – they may have spiritual or religious beliefs which allow them to accept death and dying as a natural part of human life.

Activity 14

Towards P1 and M1.
In small groups, devise a timeline which tells the story of any individual of your choice. You can give them a name and personality. At each identified life stage mention briefly the key aspects of development that they will be going through. For merit you should describe the key aspects of physical, intellectual, emotional and social development that take place at each life stage. This activity can be presented in many different ways, for example:

Continued overleaf

Activity 14 (continued)

- a poster
- a line of cards strung together
- a PowerPoint presentation
- a case history.

Using the information in section 2 for D1, in your assignment explain how the life stages identified above can be influenced.

2 Explore positive and negative influences on individuals at different life stages

Socialisation

Socialisation is a general term for the many different ways and processes by which children come to be able to function as members of their social community.

All human beings are born to be social. The rich variety of cultures in the world means that there is a lot of learning that has to happen. A large part of what goes on between parents and their children, in all cultures that have ever been studied, is to do with 'training' children in the ways of the culture. Parents teach their children not just ways of relating to others – including learning the culture's language – but also the wide variety of skills needed to function in society, for example mealtimes and rituals, bedtimes and general routines of family life.

Socialisation is quite a long, drawn-out process and in some respects it continues throughout our lifetime. Consider, for example, when adults travel abroad and interact with people from unfamiliar cultures. Even when we meet a new social group within our own culture, for example at college or in the workplace, we may need to adjust to new ways of behaving.

Activity 15

In small groups, discuss some of your family's routines and expectations. How different are they from the others in your group? You could start by considering the following:

- mealtime routines
- bedtime routines
- times to come home after being with friends (curfew)
- household tasks
- manners
- religious routines
- the way you dress.

Primary socialisation

A child begins to learn from their family group. This is where they are usually taught the values, expectations and customs of their family group and culture. It all happens from a very early age.

Secondary socialisation

Later on, children will learn about how society works from influences like teachers, the media and friends they meet. Both processes have positive and negative influences on the way we develop and see the world.

Socio-economic factors

Activity 16

Study the diagram. Discuss how each socio-economic factor can influence human growth and development both *positively* and *negatively*. Make a list of positives and negatives for each factor. Think about what factors have influenced your development. This will help you with P2 of your assignment.

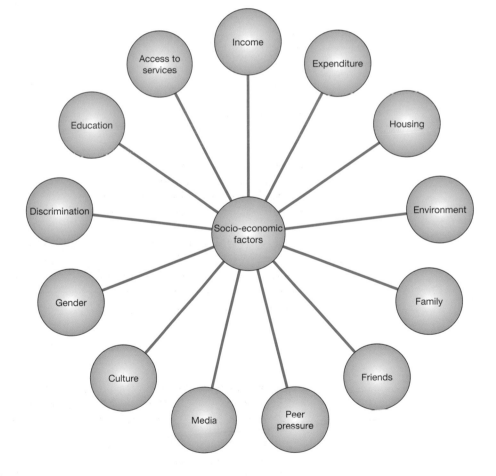

Activity 17

This will help with P2 in your assignment.

Consider the case studies below and point out what socio-economic factors have been highlighted, then suggest what positive and negative effects they may have.

Case Study 1

Judith is a single mother living in a small flat with her three-year-old son Thomas. Judith tries to budget on her low income but sometimes is forced to cut back on fresh fruit and vegetables. Sometimes she has to buy more expensive food from the local store as she cannot afford the bus fare to the supermarket where cheaper brands and offers may be available to her.

The local environment where Judith lives has high unemployment and so it is hard for her to find part-time work. She also struggles to afford suitable childcare arrangements.

She has a small, reliable network of friends.

Case Study 2

Eva and Stephan have recently moved to England from Poland with the hope of finding well-paid employment. They have been highly educated in Poland, so possess many skills.

At the moment their English-language speaking is limited. They are renting a house close to a large town. They are expecting their first child and so they need to find appropriate healthcare services and education services to support their changing lifestyle.

Case Study 3

Mark and Susan live in a large detached home in the suburbs of a town. Mark earns a high salary but his work takes him away from the family for most of the week. Susan works part time and is able to take and collect her teenage daughter Louise from high school. Their lives are extremely busy and have little routine. Susan buys a lot of convenience foods to save time on cooking but she always provides a hot meal for her daughter. Mark eats out a lot while entertaining clients in restaurants. He sometimes misses mealtimes because of his work commitments, or eats 'on the go' while travelling. Although he works very hard and is hardly ever at home, he feels it is worth it to provide money for family holidays abroad twice a year.

Activity 17 (continued)

Case Study 4

Gemma and Christopher are three-year-old twins. Their mother works full time as a nurse and their father takes care of the household and childcare duties. They have a strict routine with mealtimes and bedtime always at the same time. They all sit down together to enjoy a family meal once a day. Dad enjoys watching television while the twins are playing but Mum is worried about how this may influence the twins. They play regularly with children from next door whose rules and manners are not as strict as theirs. Occasionally the twins are confused when they see other children doing things they are not allowed to do.

Life events

During our lifetime many events will occur that may change the course of our lives. These events can be either **predictable** – we know they will happen or we choose them – or **unpredictable** – unexpected events.

Predictable life events	Unpredictable life events
Going to school/nursery	Birth of brother/sister
Employment	Divorce
Leaving home	Redundancy
Marriage	Serious injury
Parenthood	Abuse
Retirement	Bereavement
Ageing	

The effect of these life events causes short- and long-term effects. These can be stressful to the individual and to those around them. For example, can you remember when you started school or nursery? It may have been an upsetting time for you leaving your parents and your brothers and sisters. But also it may have been an exciting time, meeting new friends and playing new activities every day. For your parents it may have been a time when they could resume employment so household finances would be easier. They may have felt a sense of loss as you left for school, seeing their child grow up! It may have been a relief if they were struggling with difficult childcare arrangements.

So each life event, whether predictable or unpredictable, can bring both positive and negative effects on our lives.

Activity 18

This will help you with M2 and D2 of your assignment. Interview an older person. This could be a relative or someone from your work setting – with permission. Draw a timeline of this person's life, highlighting:

- life events – predictable or unpredictable
- how the life event affected them – positively or negatively
- what care needs did they have at this time?
- how did this affect their self-concept? (See section 3.)

Share your findings with others in your class. Compare how the same life events have affected people in different ways.

3 Examine the factors that can influence an individual's self-concept

Self-concept is your idea or picture of yourself. It is often formed from other people's opinions. Self-concept includes:

- self-esteem – our self-worth or value
- self-image – how we see ourselves in relation to others.

The way we see ourselves may be completely different to how others see us. Imagine looking at yourself in the mirror. How do you see yourself? Is it different to how other people see you?

Many factors can affect our self-concept, either positively or negatively. When a person feels good about themselves, they feel the world is a good and happy place to live in. Having a good self-concept enables us to succeed in education and society.

A person who does not feel good about themselves sees the world as an unhappy place to live. Poor self-concept may lead to fear, anxiety and low success in education and society.

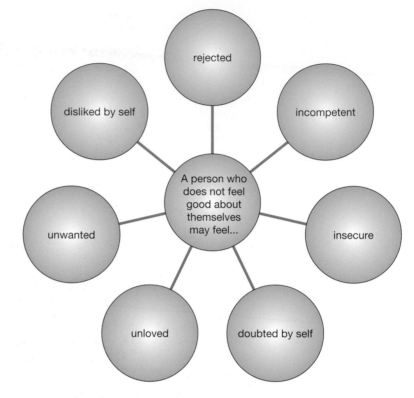

Self-concept can alter from day to day, depending on what situation you are in, and it can be influenced by many factors. Children and young people should have positive experiences around them to help their self-esteem and reinforce a positive self-image. This should enable them to be happy and active members in their society. So how can we help?

Activity 19

This will help you with P3 and M3 in your assignment.
Consider the two diagrams above: a person feeling positive and a person feeling negative about themselves. Imagine you are working with young children, in a school, nursery or at home. Some of your answers may come from your personal experiences or from your work placement experiences.
Compile a list of ideas from the following questions.

How can adults encourage positive self-image?

How can adults increase a child's self-esteem?

How can we tell that a child has a good self-concept? What signs do they give us?

Our self-concept can also be influenced by factors around us. These factors change over our life stages depending on the life events we come across.

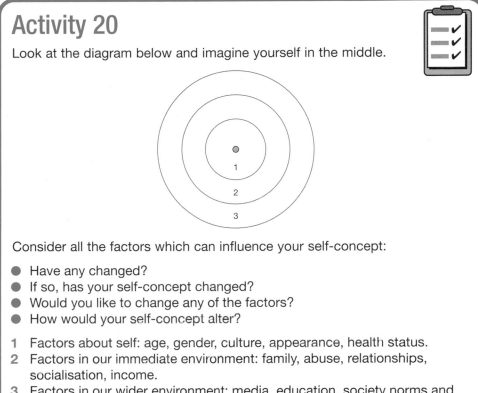

Activity 20

Look at the diagram below and imagine yourself in the middle.

Consider all the factors which can influence your self-concept:

● Have any changed?
● If so, has your self-concept changed?
● Would you like to change any of the factors?
● How would your self-concept alter?

1 Factors about self: age, gender, culture, appearance, health status.
2 Factors in our immediate environment: family, abuse, relationships, socialisation, income.
3 Factors in our wider environment: media, education, society norms and values.

4 Investigate changing care needs at different life stages

All service users need to have an identity and to feel valued. It is the role of the service provider (caregiver) to ensure this happens. As service providers we should always deliver care to our service users with **all** their needs in mind.

● **Individual care** – care that suits an individual's needs. How would you feel, as a young person, if you were admitted to hospital and you were given exactly the same care as the 65-year-old patient in the next bed to you?
● **Holistic care** – care which includes all an individual's needs. As a care worker, would it be correct to treat a young service user in the accident and emergency department with a broken leg, then send them home without asking about their home situation, work situation and mobility needs?

With these important aspects of care in mind we realise that care needs can be wide-ranging and can also differ at different life stages. (See also the care value base in Unit 1.) As care workers we need to be skilled at identifying service users' individual care needs and then planning appropriately for their care. Follow the cycle below to identify needs and plan care for individuals.

The care planning cycle

This cycle should be followed in all care establishments in some way. The Community Care Act 1990 states that all service users have the right to have their needs assessed and planned for.

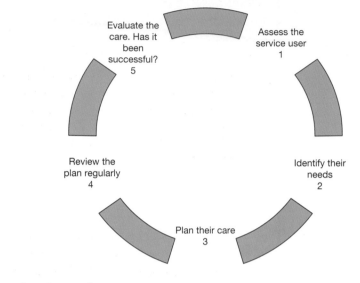

The care planning cycle

Activity 21

Investigate your work setting and see how care is assessed and planned for. Share this with your class and see how care assessments vary in different settings. Many professionals may have input into a service user's care so that all the needs are fully met. For example, a service user may see a general practitioner, a physiotherapist, a pharmacist, a nurse. This is called **multi-disciplinary care**.

Activity 22

This will help you with P4 in your assignment.
Consider the following case studies and jot down answers to these questions:

What care needs are highlighted?

How can the care be given?

What professionals should be involved?

How can meeting these care needs improve the person's self-concept?

How do the care needs vary at each life stage?

Activity 22 (continued)

Case Study 1

Mary is a 74-year-old widow who is recovering from a stroke. She is spending some time in a residential care home before returning to her own home. The stroke has left Mary slightly weakened down her left side and she occasionally needs assistance with mobility. Mary's daughter lives close by and Mary also has a good network of friends.

Case Study 2

Mohammed is 17 years old and is attending his local hospital as he is a newly diagnosed diabetic. He has been given a lot of information about his condition but is finding some of the medical terminology difficult to understand. He is going to take a friend with him to help him translate some of the information. He is very worried about his visit and how to adapt his lifestyle to his condition.

Case Study 3

Sara is about to return to work after having her first baby, Holly. Holly is 12 months old and is going to attend the local nursery. She has just started walking and enjoys playing with large wheeled toys. Sara is worried about leaving Holly as she has been used to a home environment.

Remember, we must always treat service users with dignity and respect, irrespective of their age, gender or culture.

SUMMARY

After working through this unit, you should be able to:

● identify the key aspects of physical, intellectual, emotional and social development that takes place through the life stages

● identify the positive and negative influences on growth and development

● identify factors that influence the individual's self-concept

● explain potential differences in the care needs of individuals at different life stages.

Grading grid

In order to pass this unit, the evidence that the learner presents for assessment needs to demonstrate that they can meet all of the learning outcomes for the unit. The criteria for a pass grade describe the level of achievement required to pass this unit.

Grading criteria

To achieve a pass grade the evidence must show that the learner is able to:	To achieve a merit grade the evidence must show that, in addition to the pass criteria, the learner is able to:	To achieve a distinction grade the evidence must show that, in addition to the pass and merit criteria, the learner is able to:
P1 identify the key aspects of physical, intellectual, emotional and social development that takes place through the life stages	**M1** describe the key aspects of physical, intellectual, emotional and social development that takes place through the life stages	**D1** explain how growth and development at each life stage can be influenced positively and negatively
P2 identify the positive and negative influences on growth and development	**M2** explain how life events can affect the development and care needs of individuals	**D2** explain how meeting individual care needs can improve the individual's self-concept
P3 identify factors that influence the individual's self-concept	**M3** describe how five different factors can influence the development of the individual's self-concept	
P4 explain potential differences in the care needs of individuals at different life stages		

Creative and Therapeutic Activities in Health and Social Care

This unit is about looking at how patients and service users can benefit from creative and therapeutic activities. To complete this unit you must plan, carry out and then review an activity.

Learning Outcomes

On completion of this unit you should be able to:

1 Investigate different creative and therapeutic activities appropriate to users of different health and social care settings
2 Explore the potential benefits of creative and therapeutic activities for service users
3 Examine aspects of health and safety legislation, regulations and codes of practice relevant to the implementation of creative and therapeutic activities.

1 Investigate different creative and therapeutic activities appropriate to users of different health and social care settings

There are many different activities that may have benefits for service users. Some examples are given below.

Drama therapy uses drama as part of a therapeutic process. The British Association of Drama Therapists states that drama therapy can be used to assist service users in making 'psychological, emotional and social changes'. They work in a variety of settings including schools and with a wide variety of service user groups such as children with autism or older people with dementia. For more information go to http://www.badth.org.uk.

Art can be used as a way of communicating. There is a British Association of Art Therapists (see www.baat.org) which provides more information. Art therapy can enable service users to make changes through using art materials.

Craft activities such as card making or jewellery making can be undertaken with a variety of service users.

Craft activities can be enjoyed in a variety of health and social care environments

Music may involve making music, listening to music or even music therapy, which uses music for therapeutic benefits.

Exercise may involve outdoor exercise such as walking, playing games or using the gym. Exercise has numerous benefits and can be undertaken by a variety of service users.

Writing can be used as a form of expression by service users, to enable them to communicate thoughts and feelings in a different way. It can be useful as a form of therapy.

Games and quizzes can be used by a variety of service user groups. They could be physical games such as cricket or rounders, or mental games such as quizzes or crosswords.

Yoga is described by The British Wheel of Yoga as a 'holistic approach to mind, body and spirit'. Classes generally exercise, stretch and flex the body and offer relaxation. For more information go to www.bwy.org.uk.

There are many different settings where activities may take place. Some examples are given below.

Activity 1

In pairs, discuss any work experience placements you have had in health and social care settings. What types of activities did the service users carrry out? Can you think of any creative or therapeutic activities which could be introduced into your care setting?

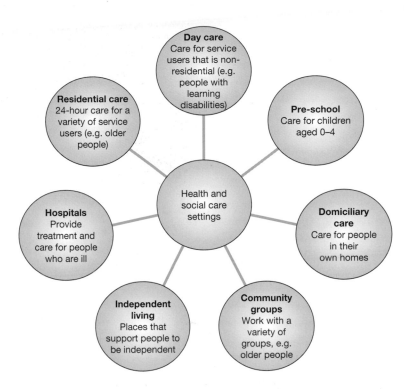

Different health and social care settings

2 Explore the potential benefits of creative and therapeutic activities for service users

Service users may have a variety of needs which may mean they could benefit from creative and therapeutic activities. These can be remembered as **PILES**! This stands for:

Physical – to do with the body. A person may have had a stroke, which could have left them with a weakness in one side of their body. Or they may have had an accident which has caused them to lose a limb. Any activities that exercise the body would count as physical.

Intellectual – to do with the brain, thinking or learning new skills. Intellectual needs may include activities that relieve boredom. They can also help prevent memory loss. Any activities that stimulate the brain or get people thinking are ideal for meeting intellectual needs.

Language – to do with how we communicate with each other. A service user could have lost the ability to speak or a child may learn new words.

Emotional – to do with how we feel about ourselves or our ability to express emotions. A service user may have poor self-esteem or may be depressed, or they may be bereaved or separated from loved ones.

Social – to do with friendship groups and working with other people. A service user could be new to the area or have few friends.

Activity 2

Read the case studies below and identify the PILES needs of those involved.

Case Studies

Sally is a 70-year-old woman. Her husband died recently and she is lonely. A lot of her friends have either moved away or died. As she is older she has poor mobility and finds it difficult to get out and about.

Nine-year-old Jodie is in hospital as she is having surgery. She sometimes finds it difficult to communicate her needs. As she has spent a lot of time in hospital she has not had the opportunity to develop many friendships with other children.

Rob has always been dependent on other carers and is now trying to increase his own independence.

When preparing an activity it is crucial to consider the needs of service users. You could find this out by asking them directly or by speaking to carers or family. You can then start to develop activities which will have maximum benefits for the individual service user. The age of the service user should be considered – different activities may suit different ages. However, it is also important to ensure that you do not make stereotypes. For example, not all older people want to play bingo!

Gender may also be a factor – generally, more men than women prefer to play football, but again, check with the individual to ensure that you are not making stereotypes. The cultural and social background of the service user should also be considered – there may be relevant factors that influence choices of activity, such as what someone can or cannot wear. Finally, the most important influence is which activities the service user would like to get involved in.

The potential benefits of creative and therapeutic activities

There are a number of benefits that service users may gain from creative and therapeutic activities. Some of these are listed below.

- New skills can be developed or existing skills can be maintained (individuals can stay physically or mentally active). Benefits could also include promoting independence or being supportive.
- Physical benefits may include improving fine motor skills such as dexterity (for example, picking up small objects) or gross motor skills, such as major muscle groups in legs or arms. Physical benefits may include a general increase in

fitness (such as in games). Physical activity is often shown to be a very important factor in good mental health as well as physical health.
- Intellectual benefits may include developing imagination (for example, making up stories), problem solving (e.g. crosswords) or developing language (such as games you may play using new words with children). Communication skills may be developed or improved.
- Emotional benefits may include improved self-esteem for the individual, or social benefits such as developing friendships and co-operation.

So why are these benefits so important? If you think about your own experiences, you will soon realise that all individuals need to engage in activities which they enjoy and which stimulate them. Service users who can communicate well, or can join in with games or play, or simply have good friends, are likely to feel more positive and happy. Some of these benefits may interlink – for example, an increase in fine motor skills and agility may improve confidence, which in turn will boost an individual's self-esteem.

Analysing the benefits of an activity

The benefits of a quiz, for example, could be:

- physical – using fine motor skills when controlling pen as writing answers.
- intellectual – using knowledge or learning new knowledge from answers known or learned.
- social – meeting new people and maintaining friendships. This also promotes a sense of co-operation and teamwork.
- emotional – may relieve boredom and can relax people, which will decrease stress levels. Also helps them express their thoughts, feelings or worries.

Activity 3

Choose one of the following activities and identify the benefits:
- playing football
- cooking
- playing a board game
- listening to a story
- playing bingo.

3 Examine aspects of health and safety legislation, regulations and codes of practice relevant to the implementation of creative and therapeutic activities

Before carrying out any activity it is crucial to consider any **health and safety implications**. This is to ensure the health and wellbeing of service users, staff, other people and the general environment. You may carry out a risk assessment which will look at what hazards there may be, what may occur as a result of this hazard and then what measures are in place to reduce the possibility of this occurring.

Example of risk assessment

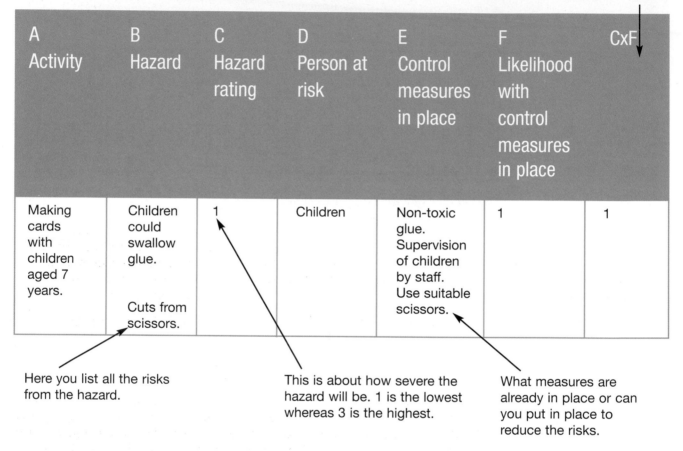

This is the probability of the risk happening with the control measures in place.

A Activity	B Hazard	C Hazard rating	D Person at risk	E Control measures in place	F Likelihood with control measures in place	CxF
Making cards with children aged 7 years.	Children could swallow glue. Cuts from scissors.	1	Children	Non-toxic glue. Supervision of children by staff. Use suitable scissors.	1	1

Here you list all the risks from the hazard.

This is about how severe the hazard will be. 1 is the lowest whereas 3 is the highest.

What measures are already in place or can you put in place to reduce the risks.

There is legislation around health and safety. A brief overview is provided below, but for more information see pages 49–51 in Unit 2.

Health and safety legislation	Brief description	Example of activities that this law may relate to
Health and Safety at Work Act 1974	Main piece of legislation covering workplaces. Both employers and employees have responsibilities to ensure health and safety.	All activities in workplaces

Health and safety legislation	Brief description	Example of activities that this law may relate to
Food Safety Act 1990 General Food Hygiene Regulations 1995	Cover all aspects of food (e.g. storage, cooking, serving).	Any activities using food, e.g. cooking
Manual Handling Operations Regulations 1992	Relates to any activities that may involve moving objects (including people).	Any activities that may involve heavy objects or moving a patient
Control of Substances Hazardous to Health 1994 (COSHH)	Ensures substances are kept safe. This includes storage, using and disposing. There should be guidelines and risk assessment in place.	Activities that involve the use of substances such as glue or paint
Reporting of Injuries Disease and Dangerous Occurrences Regulations 1995 (RIDDOR)	Ensures that accident books are monitored and completed. Certain aspects are reportable under RIDDOR.	Accident books should be kept. Any reportable occurrences should be notified to the Health and Safety Executive
Management of Health and Safety at Work Regulations 1999	Ensures that employers train staff in aspects of health and safety.	All activities in workplace

As well as these laws there may be specific policies (such as the confidentiality policy) that you should observe. There may also be other codes of practice. Before undertaking an activity you should consider any possible hazards and how the impact of these can be reduced. For example, the hazard could cause injury to the service user or to the member of staff involved. There may also be hazards in the environment or from equipment, such as when a young child using scissors would be at risk of cutting themselves – this is the hazard. Therefore they should use scissors designed for use by young children.

Activity 4

Towards P1, M1, D2.
Hannah is going to carry out an activity with Joshua, a two-year-old boy at a local nursery. She is going to work with him on a one-to-one basis to paint a picture.

1 Make a list of all the possible hazards.
2 How can the risks from these hazards be reduced?
3 Which of the health and safety laws relate to each of these hazards?

SUMMARY

● There are many different reasons for using creative and therapeutic activities and many health and social care settings where creative and therapeutic activities may take place.

● These activities may have numerous benefits for service users.

● Each activity should be tailored for use by the service user – different individuals will benefit from different activities.

● Activities may also present health and safety hazards. These should be considered and reduced as much as possible.

Grading grid

In order to pass this unit, the evidence that the learner presents for assessment needs to demonstrate that they can meet all of the learning outcomes for the unit. The criteria for a pass grade describe the level of achievement required to pass this unit.

Grading criteria

To achieve a pass grade the evidence must show that the learner is able to:	To achieve a merit grade the evidence must show that, in addition to the pass criteria, the learner is able to:	To achieve a distinction grade the evidence must show that, in addition to the pass and merit criteria, the learner is able to:
P1 produce initial drafts and final plans for two different creative/therapeutic activities for different patients/service users in a health and social care setting	**M1** explain how each creative/therapeutic activity could benefit the patient/service user	**D1** recommend ways of improving each creative/therapeutic activity, taking into account individual needs
P2 carry out and review the activities	**M2** describe how health and safety issues were addressed for each creative/therapeutic activity	**D2** explain why it was necessary to implement specific health and safety measures, linking these measures to the legislative requirements, regulations and codes of practice
P3 identify potential benefits of the creative/therapeutic activity to the patient/service user		
P4 identify the relevant legislation, regulations and codes of practice linked to health and safety for each creative/therapeutic activity		

This unit looks at health and social care provision and the difficulties that people may face in accessing these services. It also considers the benefits of health and social care services working in partnership. Lastly it explores different job opportunities within health and social care, the skills needed for these job roles and the related workforce development activities. If you are considering a career within health and social care it is important to know how services are accessed and organised. It is also important to know about the requirements of different job roles.

Learning Outcomes

On completion of this unit you should be able to:

1 Explore the organisation of health and social care service provision
2 Investigate the potential benefits of working in partnership for health and social care service provision
3 Investigate working in the health and social care sectors.

1 Explore the organisation of health and social care service provision

This section looks at key parts of health and social care provision in England, Wales and Northern Ireland. There are different sectors that make up our health and social care provision. These are:

● **Statutory** – these are services that are funded by the government. For example, the National Health Service.
● **Voluntary** – these are services that are generally funded by donations; some may receive lottery funding. (Remember that the staff usually still get paid!) Voluntary services are sometimes known as non-profit-making organisations, for example The Acorn Trust or The Alzheimer's Society.
● **Private** – these services are funded by the people who use them. People may pay into a savings scheme, an insurance policy, or they may pay as they use the service. For example, BUPA provides private healthcare.
● **Informal** – these are services provided informally by people such as family, friends or members of the community.

Activity 1

Read the following case study and identify the services provided and which of the sectors outlined on page 187 they fall into.

Case Study

Jane is a 70-year-old woman who has Alzheimer's disease. She lives in her own home. Jane's care is provided by her husband Terry, her daughter Ann, who visits her parents every day, and the We Care nursing agency, which is paid for by Terry, Jane and Ann. All the family also receive support from a local society. Jane's medical care is provided through her local GP and medical specialists.

National Health Service (NHS)

The NHS was set up in 1948. Its structure changes over time but currently it is made up of the following.

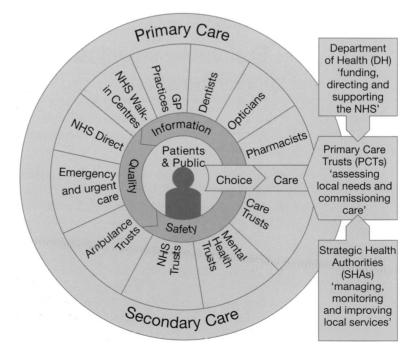

Structure of the NHS
Source: www.nhs.uk

National Service Frameworks (NSFs)

NSFs are aimed at improving specific areas of care over a long period. They are developed in partnership with a range of groups, such as health professionals, patients or voluntary organisations. There are a number of NSFs, including cancer, children, diabetes and mental health.

Primary Care Trusts (PCTs)

Primary care is the care you first receive, such as that from your GP or optician. These services are managed by the Primary Care Trust. PCTs control 80 per cent of the NHS budget (www.nhs.uk). PCTs aim to meet the needs of the local community by working with other agencies.

NHS trusts

Hospitals are managed by NHS trusts. They employ the majority of health staff and are responsible for ensuring that hospitals provide high-quality care.

Secondary healthcare

This is care that is provided following primary care, such as a referral to a specialist. An example includes a referral from your GP to a physiotherapist for a sports injury.

Mental Health trusts

These trusts are responsible for the provision of services for people with mental health problems. Some examples include counselling, specialist care or community support.

Children's trusts

Children's trusts bring together all services for children and young people in an area. They aim to improve the health outcomes for all children and young people. For more information go to www.everychildmatters.gov.uk/aims/childrenstrusts.

Integrated care

Integrated care is care provided by a number of organisations working in partnership, for example care provided for people by a health team and social services.

Social services

Social services look after people's welfare, for example the welfare of those with disabilities, or older people. Social services are run by local authorities, so each local area has its own social service office. There is often partnership between health and social services.

Activity 2

Healthcare provision is slightly different in Wales and Northern Ireland. Working in groups, research the healthcare provision using www.wales.nhs.uk or www.n-i.nhs.uk.
Compare the care provided in the different regions and discuss this with the rest of the class.

Health and social care settings

There are many different settings which provide health and social care. Each will meet different needs of different sections of the population. Some examples are shown below.

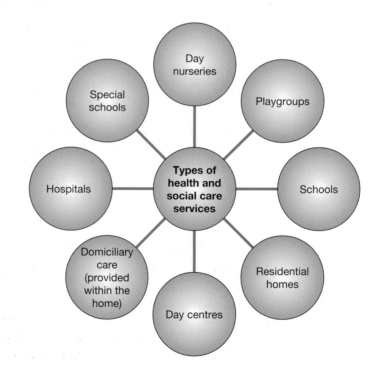

Activity 3

Make a list of all the health and social services you (or someone you know) have received.

Access (and barriers) to health and social care services

Sometimes there are barriers to accessing a health or social care service. These may be due to some of the following:

Barrier	Explanation
Specific needs	People may have particular needs – however, the specialist services that meet these needs may not be available within the local community.
Individual	People may prefer a specific service which may not be available within the local area.
Financial	Service users may not be able to afford the service or have money to get to where the service is (for example if they have to get a taxi).
Geographical	Services may be too far away or take too long to reach.
Social and cultural	There may be social or cultural needs that must be met. For example, Muslim women may prefer to be seen by a female Muslim doctor. If this was not available then this would prevent that person from accessing that service.

2 Investigate the potential benefits of working in partnership for health and social care service provision

Health and social care services are encouraged to work together. There are many examples of this. For example, multi-agency work involves a number of agencies (such as social workers and GPs) working together. Partnerships can also develop between service users and carers in planning, monitoring and reviewing care. The NHS is increasingly looking to involve other agencies and local people in planning and making decisions about the provision of health care. Primary Care Trusts may liaise with NHS trusts, social services, local universities or voluntary organisations.

Activity 4

What skills do you think NHS trusts, social services, local universities and voluntary organisations will be able to bring to a discussion on the provision of health care?

Local people can also be involved with decisions about the provision and development of local services. For more information go to www.nhs.uk/aboutnhs/howthenhsworks.

There are many reasons why different services may work in partnership. These are explained below.

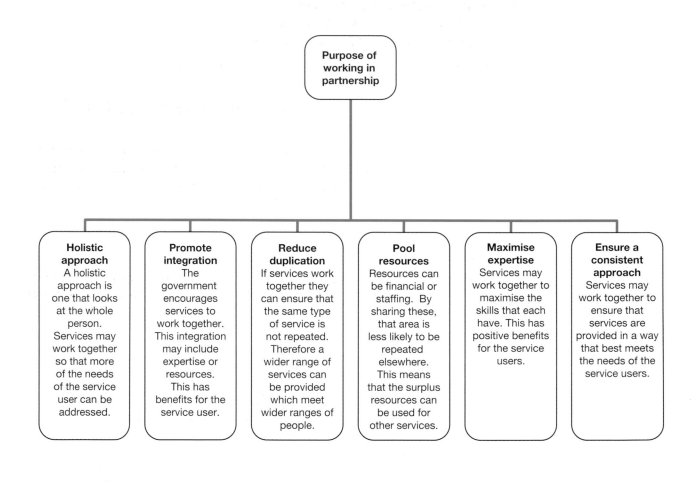

Example of partnership working

Baby Basics Project

This is a project based in Staffordshire. It is a partnership of midwives, health visitors, staff nurses and nursery nurses who provide a project to empower parents by enhancing their parenting skills.

Activity 5

What benefits do you think this project would have for the service users?

3 Investigate working in the health and social care sectors

This section looks at a wide range of job roles within health and social care. It explores the care skills and requirements of these job roles and also looks at the workforce development and guidance activities that exist.

Job roles

There are many job roles within health and social care. As well as jobs that provide hands-on care (for example nurses, doctors), there are jobs that provide support roles.

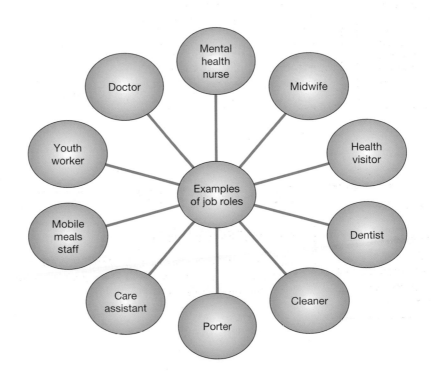

Case Study

Anthony is a social worker. Social workers work with many different groups of people, from children and families to adults with learning disabilities. Anthony works with people with mental health problems. He studied at university for three years and has a degree. He also works with a variety of other professionals such as community nurses.

Sarah is a hospital porter. She works on a shift rota system in her local hospital, moving patients around the building. Her job as a porter did not require any formal entry requirements but she has a good standard of fitness as she walks so much during the course of the day. She received a thorough induction programme when she began.

Care skills

Health and social care professionals have a variety of skills that are used in their everyday work. These include the following.

The care value base

Good care practice should reflect the care value base. It should:

● maintain confidentiality – information should not be disclosed to anyone who does not have the right to know. This helps protect service users and also builds a trusting relationship between the carers and the service user. There are exceptions to confidentiality – if the service user is in danger or there are suspicions of abuse
● promote equality and diversity – people are individuals and should be treated as individuals. Equal access should be promoted. It should also be recognised that there are many benefits to having a diverse society
● promote rights and responsibilities – all rights and responsibilities in care settings should be promoted. These include the patient's right to care that meets their needs and confidentiality.

For more information on the care value base, see Chapter 1, page 23.

Active support

Active support is about empowering people rather than doing things for them. This enables people to be as independent as possible and have control over their lives. It is about ensuring that their rights are upheld.

Interpersonal skills

Interpersonal skills are fundamental to good care practice, especially if you are working with people who may be vulnerable or frightened. This will enable service users to be able to express their feelings (such as pain or worry) and for care workers to be able to explain all the options available to them.

Meeting basic needs

There are a number of needs that everyone, including service users, have.

Activity 7

What basic needs can you think of? Make a list of basic needs for different kinds of patients, such as young children or older people.

If these basic needs are not met, this can have a detrimental impact on the health and wellbeing of service users. Some people cannot meet their basic needs themselves, especially if they are unwell. Therefore health and care workers should ensure that these needs are met whilst maintaining the rights of service users.

Maintaining personal hygiene/avoiding cross infection

When working with vulnerable or very ill patients it is important to avoid cross infection. This is where infection is passed from one person to another. This can cause dangerous infections, especially in the most vulnerable patients.

Activity 8

Research the recommended way of washing hands to avoid infection.

Requirements

There are many personal attributes that are required if you are going to work within health and social care. Most importantly, professionals should be competent and qualified for their job. Some of the key skills are examined below.

- An ability to work with others is important as you will be involved in teamwork with a variety of people, including the service user and their families/ friends and other professionals.
- Being empathetic is fundamental to a health and social care role. Empathy can be explained as the ability to recognise and identify with the feelings of another person.
- In addition it is important for staff members to have a professional attitude. They will be expected to be confident, punctual and have a positive attitude to their work.

Health and social care workers should have the necessary qualifications to perform the job and in some cases registration with a professional body is required.

Anthony (the social worker in the Case Study above) would need to have patience and empathy and be able to develop good relationships with service users. He would need good communication skills and a professional attitude. He would also have to register with the General Social Care Council. Sarah (the hospital porter) would need to have good communication skills and physical stamina. She would need the ability to stay calm. She may also have to register with the Healthcare Professionals Agency.

Workforce development

Workforce development is about improving or learning new skills. There are a number of workforce development strategies that health and social care professionals may use.

The Sector Skills Council

The Sector Skill Councils is an independent organisation. It looks at what the workforce needs and decides how these needs are going to be met. Sector Skills Agreements are then drawn up to agree how training is going to be established. The four goals are:

- to reduce skills gaps and shortages
- to improve productivity, business and public service performance
- to increase opportunities to boost the skills and productivity of everyone in the sector's workforce
- to improve learning supply, including apprenticeships, higher education and National Occupational Standards (NOS).

(*Source*: http://www.ssda.org.uk/ssda/default.aspx?page=2)

Induction

An induction is about giving a new employee an introduction to the job they will be doing. It generally includes health and safety information, the facilities in the workplace, where to go in the case of an emergency, and may also provide information about pay and conditions. This helps the new employee settle into their job and therefore better continuity of care is provided for service users.

Continuing professional development

Continuing professional development is about improving or developing skills and knowledge. This may involve training programmes or reflecting on experiences.

Transition

Transition is about managing change. An example of this could be new policies and procedures. Managers/employers will have a plan in place for how this change will be managed.

Agenda for Change

This is about making pay fairer and supporting development and progression for staff. It created a single pay system and applies directly to all employed NHS trust staff. The new pay system ensures fair pay and a clearer system for career progression. For the first time staff are paid on the basis of the jobs they are doing and the skills and knowledge they apply to these jobs.

NHS knowledge and skills framework

This is part of the Agenda for Change framework which supports the career and personal development of staff. Each staff member will have a review once a year which looks at their development in relation to knowledge and skills.

Skills escalator

The skills escalator is the structure that exists to enable all levels of the workforce to acquire new skills. This also means that staff have access to more career opportunities and provides opportunities for people to enter health and social care roles by providing a range of entry routes.

Activity 9

What ways are there to monitor performance in your workplace? How often do they happen? Who carries them out?

Ways of monitoring performance

Employees' performance is often monitored to ensure the job is being carried out competently. This can be used to enable employees to reflect on their performance and develop or improve skills. Examples of ways in which performance can be monitored are appraisals and supervisions.

Guidance

Legislation

These are laws that everyone must follow. Some examples include the Sex Discrimination Act 1975, Race Relations Act (Amendment) 2000, Health and Safety at Work Act 1974, Disability Discrimination Act 2005.

Activity 10

Get together into groups and research one of the laws mentioned above. Find out the most important parts of the law (legislation) and write a few sentences about this.

National Minimum Standards

This is a set range of requirements with which care providers such as residential homes have to abide. It came into force as part of the Care Standards Act 2000. For more information go to www.csci.org.uk.

Activity 11

What organisational policies exist within your workplace?

Organisation policies and procedures

Each organisation will have its own policies and procedures which staff should follow. These will also be in line with national legislation. Some examples may include confidentiality policy or equal opportunities policy.

Charters

Charters are expectations of what you can expect from a service or organisation and set out their aims and objectives. For example, the new NHS Charter tells people about the standards of treatment and care they can expect of the NHS. It also explains patients' responsibilities.

Codes of practice

All professions have their own code of practice. These provide guidelines on expected behaviour. Examples include the nursing code of practice (see http://www.nmc-uk.org) or the General Social Care Council code of practice for social care workers (see http://www.gscc.org.uk/Home).

Terms and conditions

Terms and conditions are generally defined as the expectations that you can have from your employer – in other words, the 'terms' on which you are employed. They may contain information about how much you will be paid, what you will be expected to do, or how much annual holiday you have. They will also contain information about disciplinary proceedings or grievance policy.

SUMMARY

- Our health and social care is provided by different care settings. These can be statutory, private, informal or voluntary.

- Accessible, affordable, appropriate provision of health and social care services is very important.

- Barriers can prevent people from accessing health and social care services. Health and care workers should be aware of barriers and should try to reduce these as much as possible.

- Health and social care service providers (agencies) work together when providing services.

- There are many reasons for this, such as pooling resources, maximising expertise or reducing duplication.

- This has positive benefits for service users as they will be receiving care from service providers with a range of experiences and expertise. Also, when resources are pooled, a wider range of services can be made available in the local area.

Grading grid

In order to pass this unit, the evidence that the learner presents for assessment needs to demonstrate that they can meet all of the learning outcomes for the unit. The criteria for a pass grade describe the level of achievement required to pass this unit.

Grading criteria		
To achieve a pass grade the evidence must show that the learner is able to:	To achieve a merit grade the evidence must show that, in addition to the pass criteria, the learner is able to:	To achieve a distinction grade the evidence must show that, in addition to the pass and merit criteria, the learner is able to:
P1 describe the key elements of health and social care service provision in a named country	**M1** use different examples to explain barriers to access of health and social care services	**D1** explain how barriers to access to services may be overcome by effective partnership working
P2 identify the factors that are potential barriers to access of health and social care services	**M2** explain how the two examples of health and social care service providers working in partnership benefit patients/service users	**D2** explain how workforce development activities help to maintain a competent health and social care workforce
P3 describe two examples of health and social care service providers working in partnership locally	**M3** explain the requirements of the two job roles	
P4 describe the requirements of two different job roles in health and social care	**M4** use examples to explain the importance of relevant guidance and workforce development activities for health and social care workers	
P5 describe the skills needed for the two job roles		
P6 describe relevant guidance and potential workforce development activities for the two job roles		

The Impact of Diet on Health

This unit explores the key principles of nutrition and how it is linked with good health. It highlights the dietary needs of individuals and looks at different requirements – for example, life stages, culture, or specific health needs. This unit also considers health problems which are linked to unbalanced diets and how they can be avoided. It provides information about safe preparation of food and hygiene practices.

Learning Outcomes

In this unit you will learn:

1 Investigate the dietary needs of individuals at different life stages
2 Examine the effects of unbalanced diets on the health of individuals
3 Investigate specific dietary needs of patients/service users
4 Explore the principles of food safety and hygiene.

1 Investigate the dietary needs of individuals at different life stages

A person's diet depends on many factors, the main one being age or life stage. A balanced diet is one that contains a variety of foods or nutrients, so the correct amounts are eaten according to the individual needs. Factors which affect our diets are discussed later in this unit.

Activity 1

Consider your diet over a day, then compare it with a toddler's diet and an elderly person's diet. What differences do you notice?

Life stages and variation during development

Infancy 0–3 years

Newborn babies are unique in that they can rely on a single food, milk, in order to meet all their nutritional needs. Breast milk is ideal for many reasons:

- It contains all nutrients in correct amounts.
- It contains antibodies which protect the newborn baby against diseases in the first few months of life.
- It is clean.
- It is in correct proportions and readily available.
- It does not cause allergies.

A mother is encouraged to breastfeed for the first few weeks of her newborn baby's life. However, some mothers are unable to breastfeed or prefer not to, therefore formula milk, which is modified cow's milk, is given. As the infant's kidneys and digestive system are immature, it is important for mothers to follow instructions on how to prepare formula feeds – this prevents the risk of infection.

4 months

When the baby is introduced to solid foods the process is called 'weaning'. This can be started around four months of age so that damage to the young kidney, as well as obesity and allergies, are avoided.

6 months

At this age, more solid foods such as cereals, pureed fruit and vegetables can be introduced. As the baby continues to grow, lumpier food can be introduced, although some babies take longer than others to learn how to chew and swallow lumps.

12–18 months

The toddler can now be given cow's milk (full fat milk) and they should be eating quite a varied diet. They will be drinking less milk as they start to eat more solid foods with the rest of the family. Skimmed milk should be given only after the age of five. Up to the age of three the diet should include iron-rich foods. Children who are weaning are also starting to move around and use more energy. Therefore their diet should contain carbohydrates, which provide a good source of energy for crawling and toddling youngsters.

Activity 2

In small groups, research which foods are rich in iron. Plan a menu which would be appropriate for a toddler (2–3 years).

Childhood 4–10 years

At this age children are active, they are actively exploring and also beginning their education, so their diet should reflect their needs. Their energy requirements will be high, but only in relation to their body size (they have smaller stomachs than an adult). This is a very important time for children's nutrition, as they will develop likes and dislikes. By encouraging healthy meals, snacks and drinks you will help children establish good eating habits for the future. Sweets, fizzy drinks, fatty and sugary foods should generally be avoided, as they can cause obesity, but they can be given occasionally, as treats. They are best given at mealtimes as this will help to avoid tooth decay. Children at this age are becoming quite independent, so you should encourage social skills such as eating with a knife and fork and drinking from a cup at a table. You should also encourage them to get into good habits of regularly brushing their teeth.

Adolescence 11–18 years

Adolescents are growing rapidly in weight and height, and many physical changes are taking place both internally and externally. These changes all require energy so an adolescent's appetite can be large – but their diet should still be well balanced. A diet high in sugar, salt and fat could lead to problems such as obesity, heart disease or diabetes in later life. Adolescents should also participate in regular physical exercise to avoid these health problems. They should be informed about the risks of severe dieting which some teenagers are susceptible to.

Adulthood 19–65 years

Adults need to maintain a healthy, well-balanced diet; it is this age group who should reduce their intake of carbohydrates and fats to avoid heart disease, obesity and diabetes. Adults' nutritional requirements do reduce with age but they should still be advised to take regular physical exercise. Adults should also be advised about the safe intake of alcohol per week:

- Women – 14 units
- Men – 21 units.

Activity 3

Investigate what a unit of alcohol is equivalent to and prepare an information poster for display in your classroom regarding safe alcohol intake levels.
This BUPA web link will help you:
http://www.bupa.co.uk/health_information/asp/healthy_living/lifestyle/alcohol/alctest.asp.

Pregnancy and breastfeeding

In teenage pregnancy girls are more likely to suffer with nutrient deficiencies as their bodies are still growing and developing, so they should eat extra nutrients to help the foetus grow and provide breast milk. During adult pregnancy and breastfeeding a woman's nutritional needs increase slightly, for the development of the foetus and the placenta and the production of breast milk. The term 'eating for two' is well known, but not entirely accurate. Rather than eating a lot more food, women should ensure their diet is nutritious and well balanced. When planning to get pregnant and during early pregnancy, women are advised to take extra folic acid in the diet or in tablet form. Folic acid has been proven to lower the risk of spina bifida in the foetus. Generally, if the mother and family have good dietary habits they will be able to pass them on to their growing children.

Old age 65+ years

As we age we become less mobile, so our energy requirements decrease slightly. Also, our bodies are not growing at the same rate as those of younger people. Although they do not need a lot of food, they still need good sources of protein, vitamins and minerals. Some older people may not eat enough or they may not have the correct balance of nutrients. This could be because they are living alone, or they lose their partner and do not feel like cooking meals for one person, or they may just lose their appetite.

In order to maintain their appetite, older people can be encouraged to cook easy, nutritious meals, possibly with extra flavourings like herbs and spices. Obviously this will help to avoid illnesses and diseases. Gentle exercise should also be promoted to help with their physical, mental and social wellbeing.

Activity 4

To check your knowledge, follow the link below, click onto different life stages and complete the activities which allow you to investigate and plan diets for the Tweedie Family. This will help you understand the diet variation during life stages. http://www.food4life.org.uk/dietary_advice.

Intake and needs

Apart from the mother's milk for her newborn infant, there is no one single food which provides enough nutrients for a healthy, balanced diet, so we depend on a variety of foods to keep us healthy. Generally there are no unhealthy foods – it is unbalanced amounts of foods which can lead to health problems. These will be discussed later on in this unit.

Dietary Reference Values

Dietary Reference Values (DRVs) were developed by the Department of Health in 1991 to replace Recommended Daily Amounts (RDAs). DRVs are benchmark intakes of energy and nutrients – they can be used for guidance but should not be seen as exact recommendations. They show the amount of energy or an individual nutrient that a group of people of a certain age range (and sometimes sex) needs for good health.

Although DRVs are given as daily intakes, people often eat quite different foods from one day to the next and their appetite can change, so, in practice, the intakes of energy and nutrients need to be averaged over several days. Also, DRVs apply only to healthy people.

DRV is a general term used to cover the following:

- **Estimated average requirement (EAR)**: the average amount of energy or a nutrient needed by a group of people.
- **Reference nutrient intake (RNI)**: the amount of a nutrient that is enough to meet the dietary needs of about 97 per cent of a group of people.
- **Lower reference nutrient intake (LRNI)**: the amount of a nutrient that is enough for a small number of people in a group with the smallest needs. Most people will need more than this.
- **Safe intake**: this is used when there is not enough evidence to set an EAR, RNI or LRNI. The safe intake is the amount judged to be enough for almost everyone, but below a level that could have undesirable effects.

The Balance of Good Health

The Food Standards Agency (FSA) has given us 'Eight Guidelines for a Healthy Diet' (source: www.food.gov.uk), from which is derived The Balance of Good Health. This aims to convey a practical message about healthy eating and will hopefully reduce the confusion about what healthy eating really means. The appearance of The Balance of Good Health in a number of settings, such as health centres, supermarkets, schools and workplaces, will help to maintain a consistent message.

The Balance of Good Health suggests:

- Enjoy your food.
- Eat a variety of different foods.
- Eat the right amount to be a healthy weight.
- Eat plenty of foods rich in starch and fibre.
- Eat plenty of fruit and vegetables.
- Don't eat too many foods that contain a lot of fat.
- Don't have sugary foods and drinks too often.
- If you drink alcohol, drink sensibly.

It is based on five **food groups**:

● Fruit and vegetables – to provide a variety of nutrients such as carbohydrates for energy, vitamin C to help heal wounds, and fibre. The aim is to eat a variety of five a day.
● Bread, other cereals and potatoes – to provide energy from carbohydrates and fibre. The aim is to eat this in good amounts at every meal.
● Milk and dairy – to provide calcium, protein necessary for growth and repair, and vitamin D which helps calcium and phosphate absorption and healthy teeth and bones. These should be eaten in moderate amounts and where possible lower-fat alternatives should be used (except for babies and young children).
● Meat, fish and alternatives – this group provides iron, protein and zinc necessary for the growth of tissues. These should be eaten in moderate amounts and lower-fat alternatives should be used where necessary.
● Foods containing fat and sugar – this group of foods provides fats and carbohydrates. It is recommended to eat these in small amounts.

The 5-a-day campaign aims to encourage people to eat a variety of fruit and vegetables every day. Different amounts of fruit or vegetables count as one portion.

1 medium apple

2 broccoli florets

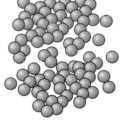

3 heaped tablespoons of peas

7 strawberries

16 okra

1 medium glass of orange juice

Examples of 5-a-day fruit and vegetables
Source: http://www.5aday.nhs.uk

Have a look at www.5aday.nhs.uk. This campaign aims to change the way we all think about fruit and vegetables, and to encourage us to eat at least five portions a day. Eating a healthy diet of fruit and vegetables provides a range of vitamins, minerals and nutrients, and can reduce the risk of heart disease and strokes.

Malnutrition and nutrient deficiencies

The term **malnutrition** means unbalanced eating habits which in time can lead to health conditions. It can also relate to **under-nutrition** or **over-nutrition**. **Under-nutrition** is mainly linked to the less developed countries where there is not enough food for the whole population. A long-term lack of protein, carbohydrates and other nutrients can cause disorders such as marasmus or kwashiorkor. Young children and old people are most at risk from serious starvation. Under-nutrition in a developed country such as the UK is relatively rare, since there is generally plenty of food to go round. Iron deficiency is an example of under-nutrition and can lead to anemia. **Over-nutrition** is mainly linked to developed countries where there is excessive consumption of food. This can cause disorders such as obesity, heart disease, tooth decay or liver damage. (These are discussed later in the unit.)

Components of a balanced diet

As part of a balanced diet there are five main groups of nutrients:

- protein
- fat
- carbohydrates
- vitamins
- minerals.

Fluid is also needed in the diet to survive.

Nutrients can be split into two groups:

1   **Macro nutrients** (macro means large/big). These are needed in our body in large amounts. They are proteins, fats and carbohydrates.
2   **Micro nutrients** (micro means small). These are needed in small amounts in our body. These are vitamins and minerals.

Micronutrients	
Vitamins	**Minerals**
Thiamin	Calcium
Riboflavin	Phosphorus
Niacin	Iron
B6	Magnesium
B12	Sodium
Folate	Potassium
Vitamin C	Chloride
Vitamin A	Zinc
Vitamin D	Copper
Vitamin E	Selenium
Vitamin K	Iodine
	Molybdenum
	Cobalt
	Manganese
	Chromium
	Fluoride

Carbohydrates

There are two main types of carbohydrates: sugar and starch.

Sugar

This is found in foods like jams, sweets, honey and soft drinks. Sugar is also added to desserts, cakes and biscuits. Sugar contains monosaccharide (simple sugars) and disaccharides (complex or double sugars).

Some names of monosaccharides are:

- Fructose
- Galatose
- Glucose.

Some names of disaccharides are:

- Sucrose
- Lactose
- Maltose.

Activity 5

In small groups, investigate these names and uncover more information about them.
Find out what foods they are present in and what they are used for in the body. Present your information as a poster or in table format.

Starch

This is found in foods like bread, potatoes, rice and pasta. Starches are called polysaccharides (poly means many), which means starch is made up of many units of monosaccharide (single sugars). Non-starch polysaccharides are more commonly known as cellulose or dietary fibre. This is found in foods like vegetables, fruit and cereals (it used to be called roughage). It is fibrous and cannot be digested by humans but it does have many health benefits. It encourages us to chew our food thoroughly, it adds bulk to the diet so encourages our digestive tract to work effectively, it helps to avoid constipation and may prevent some bowel disorders and diseases.

Activity 6

A sports person may require more carbohydrates in their diet. Can you suggest reasons why?

Sugar and starch carbohydrates both provide equal amounts of energy, but starch carbohydrates are the healthier option. Sugar carbohydrates are strongly linked with tooth decay. Carbohydrates are needed in our diet to provide our main source of energy. Experts have estimated that over half the energy in our diets should come from carbohydrates.

Proteins

Proteins are essential in our diet and are used in the body for repair and growth of new cells in the body. The immune system, which fights infection, is also made up of protein. Therefore it is really important that groups of people like babies, children, the elderly and ill people in particular have a regular supply of protein in their diets. Protein is found in a range of foods, the main sources being red meat, poultry, fish, eggs, milk and yoghurt. Obviously vegetarians (who do not eat meat or fish) need their supply from other foods, such as nuts, pulses (peas, beans and lentils), mushrooms and some vegetables. Vegans also need to be very careful about including good sources of protein in their diet.

Proteins are made up of building blocks which are called amino acids. Some of these amino acids are called 'essential amino acids'. These have to be supplied by diet. There are eight essential amino acids:

- Isoleucine
- Phenlalanine
- Leucine
- Threonine
- Lysine
- Tryptophan
- Methionine
- Valine.

Activity 7

Phenylketonuria (PKU) is a genetic disorder that is characterised by the body's inability to use the essential amino acid phenylalanine. PKU is a rare disorder which can cause brain damage in severe cases. It can be detected by a blood test (heel prick) around eight days after birth and can be treated by a special diet. Investigate what foods contain phenylalanine – look in your kitchen cupboards at home.

Fats

Fat is required in the diet to help to build cells in the body. It provides energy and helps with the absorption of Vitamins A, D, E and K into the body. It also provides taste and texture to food.

- **Saturated fats** are found in foods such as milk, cream, full fat cheese, lard and butter. These are less healthy fats and are sometimes called animal fats, which if eaten in excess can cause heart disease.
- **Polyunsaturated fats** are found in foods such as soya oil, corn and fish. These are classed as fats which help our body.
- **Monosaturated fats** are found in olive oil and are said to benefit the heart. A lot of unsaturated fats come from plant oils.

- **Essential fatty acids** are polyunsaturated fats which cannot be made by the body so have to be provided by the diet. They help to build cells. **Omega 3 Fats** can help prevent heart disease and are helpful in joint diseases – they can be found in oily fish. **Omega 6 Fats** can help prevent heart disease as they reduce cholesterol levels. They can be found in sunflower oil, corn oil, soya oil, cereal, eggs and poultry.

Vitamins

Vitamins are essential in a healthy diet – they help with metabolic functions in the body.

Vitamin comes from the word 'vital'. They are needed in the body in very small amounts and different age groups and genders require different amounts to stay healthy.

There are two types of vitamins: fat-soluble and water-soluble vitamins.

Fat-soluble vitamins are stored in the liver and do not have to be taken in every day. They are vitamins A, D, E and K. **Water-soluble vitamins** cannot be stored in the body so should be taken in daily. They are the vitamin B group and C. The chart below shows the sources, function and requirement for vitamin intake (fat-soluble in red, water-soluble in blue).

Vitamin	Sources	Role in the body and effect of shortage
A (Retinol)	Animal foods, milk, cheese, eggs, oily fish, fruit and vegetables. In animal products it is known as retinols and plant carotenes (which the body converts to retinol).	Essential for vision in dim light. A prolonged lack can lead to night blindness. It helps with the maintenance of healthy skin and keeps mucous membranes (such as eyes and throat) free from infection, supple and smooth. It also assists in the growth of bones and teeth and helps the body fight infection. Too much Vitamin A can lead to a toxic effect as the liver cannot process it. There is also a link between too much Vitamin A and birth defects. As a consequence pregnant women are advised not to take nutritional substances which contain Vitamin A.
D (Cholecalci-ferol)	Found in fish liver oils, oily fish, eggs, dairy products, and is added to margarine by law. It is also found in the UV rays in sunlight. Vitamin D is stored in the liver and can be used as required.	Required for bones and teeth - these contain large amount of calcium and phosphorus. Vitamin D helps the absorption of calcium. People are unlikely to be deficient in Vitamin D unless they have limited exposure to the sun. Lack of Vitamin D can cause weak bones and teeth, Bones may then bend, which can cause rickets in children or osteomalacia in adults. Too much, though, can lead to deposits of calcium in the joints, which can damage organs.

Vitamin	Sources	Role in the body and effect of shortage
C (Ascorbic Acid)	Fresh fruit and vegetables fruit juices	Aids absorption of iron and helps build bones and teeth. It aids Vitamin E as an antioxidant and is necessary to build and maintain skin and digestive system. Helps fight infection by protecting immune systems. Shortage can lead to scurvy and poor healing of damaged cells.
B1 – Thiamin	Milk, eggs, vegetables, fruit	Helps release energy from carbohydrates. Shortage causes beri beri (linked with alcoholism), depression, pins and needles.
B2 – Riboflavin	Milk and milk products	Helps utilise energy from foods. Shortage causes sore mouth and tongue.
B3 – Niacin	Cheese, meat (especially chicken)	Helps utilise food energy. Shortage causes skin peeling, diarrhoea, memory loss, insomnia.
B6 – Pyridoxine	Meat, fish, eggs	Metabolism of amino acids and helps form haemoglobin. Shortage causes nerve problems and fatigue.
B12 – Cyanocobal-amin	Meat (especially liver) milk, eggs, cheese. Does not occur in vegetables.	Needed by cells that divide rapidly. One example is bone marrow, which helps make red blood cells. Shortage causes pernicious anaemia and degeneration of nerve cells.
Folate (Folic acid)	Leafy green vegetables, potatoes and oranges	Helps Vitamin B12 with rapidly dividing cells. Important in pregnancy. Shortage may cause anaemia.
E (Tocopherol)	Vegetable oils, nuts and egg yolk	Major role as an antioxidant. Stored in the body to protect body cell from free radicals (unstable compounds that damage healthy body cells). It also maintains a healthy reproductive system, nerve and muscles. Shortage causes muscle and cell function.
K	Widespread in many foods including leafy vegetables such as spinach, cauliflower, it can be produced in the body by bacteria.	Essential for blood clotting. Babies tend to be given an injection of Vitamin K at birth. Shortage is rare, and is usually in babies, called Vitamin K deficiency bleeding.

Minerals

Minerals are split into essential minerals and trace minerals. Below is a chart showing the sources and roles of essential minerals in the body.

Mineral	Sources	Role in the body and effect of shortage
Calcium	Milk, cheese, eggs, bones of canned fish and is added to white flour by law.	Calcium combined with phosphorous gives strength to teeth and bones; it helps with blood clotting and nerve functioning. Shortage causes poor teeth development, rickets in children and osteomalacia in adults. Tetany may result if muscles and nerves do not function properly.
Phosphorous	Present in all natural foods	It is an important part of producing energy in the body and helps make bones strong. Shortage is very rare.
Iron	Red meat, offal, fish, dark leafy green vegetables, pulses, cereal, nuts, dried herbs and spices.	Iron carries oxygen in the blood to all cells. Vitamin C helps the body absorb more iron. Shortage causes anaemia, particularly infants 6–12 months, teenage girls who are menstruating and the elderly.
Magnesium	All green vegetables and red meat	Important for the development of the skeleton and nerve function. Shortage causes leg cramps, slow body growth, confusion.
Sodium	Found in many additives, snacks and preservatives, naturally found in eggs, meat and vegetables.	Helps to maintain fluid balance with potassium and chloride sodium. Important for nerve and muscle impulses. Shortage causes muscle cramps, excessive amounts can lead to high blood pressure.
Potassium	Bananas, all other fruit and vegetables	Like sodium helps to maintain fluid balance, can help to reduce blood pressure and the functioning of heart muscles. Severe shortage causes heart failure.
Chloride	Olives, lettuce, tomatoes and celery	As the two minerals above, helps with fluid balance and with sodium is table salt. Shortages are not common but excessive amounts can cause fluid retention.
Zinc	Meat, cheese, eggs, fish, pulses and cereals	Helps with fighting diseases and infections, helps with wound healing, also the production of sperm. Is part of many enzymes. Shortages cause enzyme disorders.

Activity 8

Write a list of all the meals you had yesterday. Break down what you have eaten in terms of the nutrients.
Do you notice any foods you are lacking in?
Do you notice any foods you are having too much of?
How does your diet compare to that of your class members?

All the above information will help you with P1, M1 and D1 of your assignment. Link the information you have learned about a balanced diet to life stages. For example, the needs of a newborn baby are very different to the needs of an elderly person. Remember, diet is not just what nutrients you have but the amount you have, the frequency you have them and the method with which you serve them. Again, a baby of six months may eat pureed vegetables, whereas an adult may eat raw or steamed vegetables.

Factors influencing the diet of individuals

Activity 9

As a class, produce a 'thought shower' of words and sentences which explains what affects your choice of diet. Try to explain your answers. Some ideas are listed in the diagram – you will probably come up with many more. This activity will help you to investigate P2 of your assignment.

Religion/culture

In our diverse society, culture and religion play a large part in food choices. Certain foods may be accepted by one member of the family and not by another, even if they share the same background, culture and religion. In other words, people have different tastes. As with vegetarians, people may make different choices, according to ethical or religious reasons, or just personal likes or dislikes.

Investigate the following groups and identify their dietary rules regarding their religion or culture:

- Hindus
- Jews
- Muslim
- Sikh
- Buddhist
- Vegetarian
- Vegan.

Social class

There is some evidence that different social classes may also have different dietary choices. This could be a good group discussion. It may be said that people from higher social classes eat a healthier diet because they have been well educated and can afford fresh meat and vegetables. Therefore, it may be argued that people from a lower social class with less money have a poorer diet because of a lower income.

On the other side of this debate, people in a higher social class who have highly paid jobs with travel and stress involved may eat very rich meals, but sometimes an unhealthy diet.

What do you think? Discuss these points as a class. You may want to consider: is organic food more expensive? What about so-called 'fast food': is this really cheaper?

Personal preferences

Obviously personal preference influences dietary choices. This is not just about taste, likes and dislikes but can also be linked to habits. For example, having breakfast may or may not be a habit and it may be difficult to change this habit later on in life. As we have seen, food choices may also be linked to religion or culture. For example, it may be your personal preference not to eat meat, or it may be part of your religion.

Peer pressure

This means that your dietary choices may be influenced by those around you. It usually relates to children and teenagers. Obviously these choices may be healthy or unhealthy.

The media

Information in the media such as television adverts, magazine articles, leaflets, posters and soap operas on television, published research articles and news events all have an influence on our food choices, although we sometimes don't realise it.

Activity 10

Think of some food-related articles in the media and discuss how they may have influenced people's food choices. A few ideas to get you started include the following:

● Did the recent cases of bird flu affect how you feel about purchasing or consuming certain animal products?

● What about the recent debates on advertising of food during children's television programmes? Are certain unhealthy foods targeted at children? Have you heard of 'pester power'?

● Could healthier foods be made more attractive to children and young people? How would you do this?

Position in family

The position in the family may determine your dietary choices for various reasons. Mothers may be seen to give larger portions to the head of the family, or the person who is responsible for the shopping may make food choices for the rest of the family. For religious and cultural reasons your choices as a baby or young child are usually made for you, until you have an understanding of that religion or culture to make your own choice.

Geographic location

This may relate to how close you live to shops or supermarkets. For example, if you live in a rural area your choice of shopping may be limited to a small local store, but you may also have a plentiful supply of fresh produce, whereas if you live in an urban area your choice of food may be much wider. Some urban areas have shops selling a wide range of healthy, organic produce, other urban areas may only have fast-food outlets or small convenience stores.

Geographic location also relates to the country where you live. A wealthy country can provide a wide variety of food and can import wider choices of foods, so seasonal foods may be available all year round. A poor country may suffer from extremes of weather, so crops may be destroyed, or food may be of low quality or limited supply. In extreme cases in less developed countries, there may be starvation when a crop fails or when families simply cannot buy enough food.

Availability of food

This could be linked to geographical location but is also to do with access and transport. Large supermarkets are usually on out-of-town estates and transport is needed to access them. Sometimes the elderly or disabled may be unable to get to them, even if public transport is available, and carrying and storage may still be a problem.

Financial resources

This is a large factor which affects our dietary choices. Groups of people who have a very limited budget may have less choice in their diet. High earners may be able to afford rich diets and expensive meals out in restaurants (but as discussed earlier, this can be either an advantage or disadvantage).

Activity 11

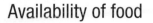

This will help you with P2 of your assignment.
Get into small groups in your class. Discuss and then describe five socioeconomic influences which may affect the following groups of people. Try to explain why.

- Teenage boy just started at university.
- Elderly lady living by herself in the country.
- Hindu family living in an underdeveloped country.
- A family of five living in a high-rise flat with no local transport, both parents working full time and children at school all day.
- Middle-class Indian family of three living in a large, detached property with two cars; father works away whilst mother is at home with a young child.

---

2 Examine the effects of unbalanced diets on the health of individuals

Unbalanced diets have a detrimental effect on our health. They can cause:

- malnutrition
- over-nutrition – CHD, obesity, type 2 diabetes
- under-nutrition – marasmus and kwashiorkor
- nutrient deficiency – anaemia, rickets, tooth decay, night blindness, beri beri, scurvy.

For P3 and M2 in your assignment, identify two of the above medical terms and describe how an unbalanced diet can lead to these conditions.

Malnutrition

This term means unbalanced or disordered eating and can be linked to under-or over-eating of particular nutrients over a long period of time, which can result in illness or disease.

Over-nutrition

This is more likely to happen in developed countries with over-consumption of fatty foods, which can result in conditions such as the following.

Coronary heart disease

Coronary heart disease is the term that describes what happens when your heart's blood supply is blocked, or interrupted, by a build-up of fatty substances in the coronary arteries. Over time, the walls of your arteries can become furred up with fatty deposits. This process is known as atherosclerosis and the fatty deposits are called atheroma. If your coronary arteries become narrow, due to a build-up of atheroma, the blood supply to your heart will be restricted. This can cause angina (chest pains).

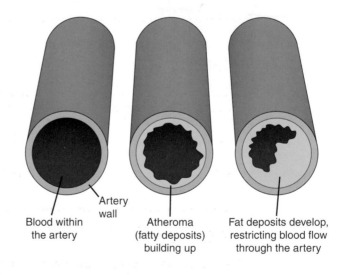

How atheroma builds up in the arteries

Obesity

Obesity is more than just a few extra pounds gained in weight. Obesity is the heavy accumulation of fat in your body to such a degree that it rapidly increases your risk of various diseases. It can damage your health and cause death from conditions such as heart disease and diabetes.

For medical purposes, the body mass index (BMI) is used to determine whether your weight is in the healthy range. Go to http://www.eatwell.gov.uk/healthissues/obesity/ to discover information about BMI and how to calculate it using a special formula and web calculator.

Type 2 diabetes

In this type of diabetes the receptors on cells in the body that normally respond to the action of insulin fail to be stimulated by it – this is known as insulin resistance. In response to this, more insulin may be produced, and this overproduction exhausts the insulin-manufacturing cells in the pancreas. There is simply insufficient insulin available and the insulin that is available may be abnormal and so doesn't work properly.

Activity 12

This will help you with P3 M2 in your assignment.
Research the above three conditions and produce a poster highlighting the signs and symptoms of these conditions and what happens if the condition continues.

Under-nutrition

This occurs mainly in underdeveloped countries where problems such as marasmus and kwashiorkor are seen. It results from too little dietary energy and proteins.

Marasmus: inadequate energy and protein intake; associated with severe wasting.

Kwashiorkor: fair-to-normal energy intake, but inadequate protein.

Activity 13

Marasmus and kwashiorkor are due to a severe lack of protein and energy in the diet. Investigate them both and highlight the differences and similarities between the two. Use a table to highlight your information.

Nutrient deficiency

Continued long-term shortage of some important nutrients can cause diseases and disorders.

Activity 14

In small groups, choose one of the disorders listed below and find out what nutrient causes the deficiency and what the characteristics of the disorder are. You could produce your findings in a poster for your classroom or an information leaflet for your colleagues.

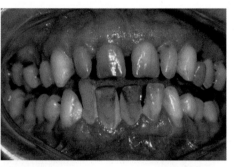

Tooth decay

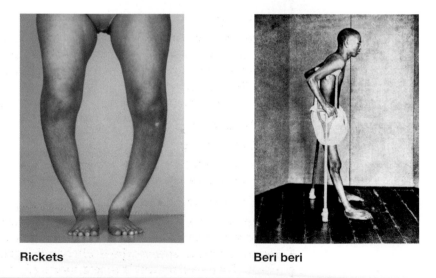

Rickets

Beri beri

3 Investigate specific dietary needs of patients/service users

Some service users have particular needs, which means they have to eat a special diet. This could be for a number of reasons.

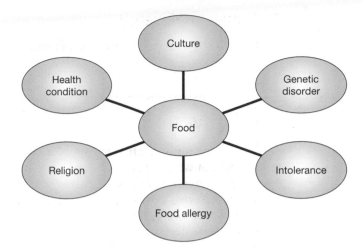

Culture

Health condition

Genetic disorder

Food

Religion

Intolerance

Food allergy

Reasons for specific dietary needs

Activity 15

Discuss all of these dietary needs as a class. In small groups, take one of the above categories and list some examples which belong to each dietary need. Then choose one example and investigate what dietary changes would have to be made to care for a service user who had this particular need.

Towards P4, M3 and D2.
Try to use some examples from your work experience to help you with this part of your assignment. Think of **two** service users, each with a specific dietary requirement from the information above, then make a two-day diet plan for each service user.
Your two-day plan should include the following:

● Breakfast and a drink
● Mid-morning snack and drink
● Midday meal and drink
● Mid-afternoon snack and drink
● Evening meal and drink.

When planning your menu, remember your service user's personal needs and preferences. Make sure that your menu is suitable and appropriate. In a report, describe why you have chosen the menus for each of the service users. Then explain why it meets their individual dietary needs.

4 Explore the principles of food safety and hygiene

Food hygiene is the action taken to ensure food is handled, stored and cooked in a way and under such conditions that as far as possible food contamination is prevented.

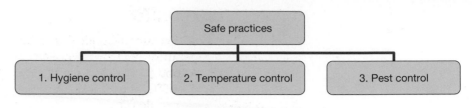

Safe practices

Hygiene control

This means to use practices which reduce the risk of food contamination. The aim is to prevent the spread of bacteria. Contamination may occur by **direct** or **indirect** contact. **Direct** is close or actual contact with the source of contamination; **indirect** is more common and can occur when something transfers the bacteria to the food, for example, hands, clothes, utensils or equipment.

Methods of food contamination

- Food-to-food contamination – raw meat to cooked meat.
- Equipment-to-food contamination – unclean surfaces where equipment stands, equipment not cleaned between uses, cloths for wiping surfaces are moved from area to area.
- Food handler-to-food contamination – use of fingers to test food, improper hand washing and personal hygiene routines.
- Others – food left to stand, not stored correctly, is contaminated by pests.

Activity 16

Choose one of the areas shown in the spider diagram below to create an information leaflet/poster which will give service providers visual and written information about personal hygiene.

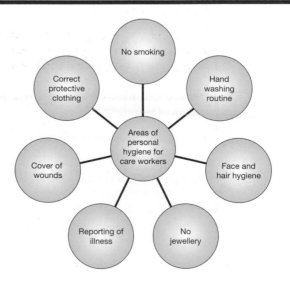

Temperature control

Bacteria will grow if they are given ideal conditions – food, warmth, moisture and time. Correct temperature control is an extremely powerful weapon against the infection of food by food poisoning bacteria. Remember, temperature danger zone is between –5°C and 63°C. Bacteria do not generally grow below –5°C or above 63°C. So follow these simple rules:

- Keep hot food hot.
- Keep cold food cold.
- Keep prepared foods out of the temperature danger zone.

Pest control

Pests eat and spoil food and are responsible for the transfer of bacteria to food.

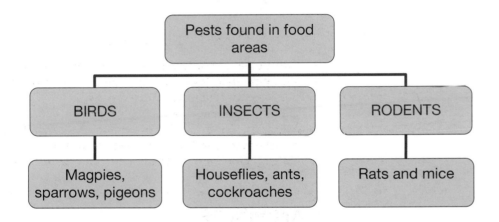

Examples of pests that may be found in food areas

Activity 17

Discuss in small groups how best to control or prevent contamination of food by pests in your working environment. You may have seen some methods enforced in your work placement.

Effects of unsafe practice

If we ignore our safe practices we are likely to suffer the effects. These can be dangerous and can cause illness and even death, particularly to vulnerable service users like children and elderly.

> ## Case Study: E. coli outbreak in Scotland update
>
> Wednesday 15 August 2007
>
> NHS Greater Glasgow and Clyde is leading an investigation into an outbreak of *E. coli* 0157 in the Paisley area. Its Public Health Protection Unit is working closely with other organisations, including the Food Standards Agency Scotland (FSAS), Renfrewshire Council and Health Protection Scotland, to identify the source of this infection.
>
> FSAS is involved in the Outbreak Control Team and will offer advice as required to assist the investigation. So far, a 66-year-old woman has died as a result of contracting the infection and her husband, aged 72, is seriously ill in hospital. A 71-year-old woman is unwell but stable in hospital in Paisley; a woman from Paisley holidaying in Ireland has been hospitalised. Four other cases are recovering at home.
>
> *E. coli* 0157 is spread in a number of ways, including eating or drinking contaminated food or drink, direct or indirect contact with infected animals and person-to-person contact.
>
> *Source:* http://www.food.gov.uk/news/newsarchive/2007/aug/ecoliresponse070814

Types of food contamination

- **Biological** – contamination of food by harmful organisms which can multiply and cause illness and disease.
- **Chemical** – contamination of food by cleaning products left near food or spilt over food.
- **Physical** – contamination of food by objects being accidentally dropped into food, for example glass, fingernails, hair dirt or insect droppings.

Bacterial food poisoning

Using the web link to The Food Standards Agency (http://www.eatwell.gov.uk/healthissues/foodpoisoning/abugslife), find out the types of bacterial food poisoning that are common, how they grow and how they affect our service users. Under 'Food poisoning', click on 'food bugs and what to do'.

Activity 18

This will help you with P5 and M4 in your assignment.
Prepare an article for a newspaper or journal and identify safe
practices for preparing, cooking and serving food. Include
a description of what could happen if these safe practices are ignored.

Legislation, regulations and codes of practice

Food Safety Act 1990

This Act covers anyone who deals with food, from farmers right through to the
catering and restaurant trade. The Act protects the person buying the food
(consumer) from poor hygiene standards and poor grades of food, and also food
which has not been labelled correctly. The Act allows local authorities to enforce
laws and give out penalties if the laws are broken.

Food Safety (General Food Hygiene) Regulations 1995

These regulations specify standards for the structural requirements for the premises,
equipment, personal safety and wholesomeness of the food. These regulations apply
to food businesses, not farms or abattoirs.

Food Safety (Temperature Control) Regulation 1995

These regulations require foods which are likely to allow the growth of pathogenic
micro-organisms or bacteria to be held at or below 8° Celsius or above 63° Celsius.
The regulations allow certain tolerances from the requirements (consistent with the
need to ensure food safety), to take into account practical considerations relating,
for example, to processing or handling.

Hazard Analysis Critical Control Point (HACCP)

HACCP is a system used by the food industry to ensure that all food consumed is
safe to eat. HACCP is a systematic approach to hazard identification and assessment
of risk and control. When implemented correctly, it ensures that every step in the
process to grow, harvest, prepare and market foods for export results in food that is
safe to eat. Thus, whether the produce comes from a smallholder or a commercial
farm, it will be safe to eat if it has been routed through an HACCP-controlled
process.

Activity 19

Find out how these regulations apply to care workers and service users in your work placement. Try to ask those staff who deal with food preparation and serving. Share your information as a class. Do they have any policies which relate just to that specific setting? What other policies and procedures do they follow? Do the regulations and policies differ from setting to setting?

SUMMARY

After working through this unit you should be able to:

● identify how the components of a balanced diet vary according to the life stage of the individual

● describe the influence of five socio-economic factors on the diet of the individual in society

● identify two medical conditions related to unbalanced diets

● produce a two-day diet plan for service users with specific dietary needs

● identify the safe practices necessary in preparing, cooking and serving food.

Grading grid

In order to pass this unit, the evidence that the learner presents for assessment needs to demonstrate that they can meet all of the learning outcomes for the unit. The criteria for a pass grade describe the level of achievement required to pass this unit.

Grading criteria

To achieve a pass grade the evidence must show that the learner is able to:	To achieve a merit grade the evidence must show that, in addition to the pass criteria, the learner is able to:	To achieve a distinction grade the evidence must show that, in addition to the pass and merit criteria, the learner is able to:
P1 identify how the components of a balanced diet vary according to life stage of the individual	**M1** describe how the components of a balanced diet contribute to an individual's health at different life stages	**D1** explain why the components of a balanced diet vary according to life stage of the individual
P2 describe the influence of five socio-economic factors on the diet of individuals in society	**M2** describe how unbalanced diets can result in the development of the two identified medical conditions	**D2** explain how the two-day diet plan meets the dietary needs of the patients/service users
P3 identify two medical conditions related to unbalanced diets		
P4 produce a two-day diet plan for two patients/service users with specific dietary needs	**M3** describe why the identified specific dietary needs require dietary adjustment for the two patients/service users	
P5 identify the safe practices necessary in preparing, cooking and serving food	**M4** describe the effects of unsafe practices when preparing, cooking and serving food	

References and Useful Websites

Gibbs, G. (1988) *Learning by Doing. A Guide to Teaching and Learning Methods*, Further Education Unit, Oxford Polytechnic.

Mehrabian, A. (1971) *Silent Messages*, Belmont, California: Wadsworth.

Moonie, N., Bates, A. and Spencer-Perkins, D. (2004) *Diversity and Rights in Care* (*Care Management Series*), Heinemann.

O'Brien, M. (2000) 'Adults with a Psychotic Disorder Living in Private Households, 2000', London: HMSO.

O'Hagan, K. (2001) *Cultural Competence in the Caring Professions*, Jessica Kingsley.

Skelt, A. (1993) *Caring for People with Disabilities*, Pearson.

Thomas, B. and Dorling, D. (2007) *Identity in Britain: A cradle-to-grave atlas*, The Policy Press.

www.audit-commission.gov.uk: Audit Commission

www.bbc.co.uk: BBC

www.bcodp.org.uk: British Council for Disabled People

www.bupa.co.uk: BUPA

www.businessballs.com: Business Balls.com

www.ccwales.org.uk: Care Council for Wales

www.careknowledge.com: Care Knowledge

www.community-care.co.uk: Community Care

www.csci.org.uk: Commission for Social Care Inspection

www.doh.org: Department of Health

www.eoc.org.uk: Equal Opportunities Commission

www.equalityhumanrights.com: Equality and Human Rights Commission

www.gscc.org.uk: General Social Care Council

www.hse.gov.uk: Health and Safety Executive

http://intute.ac.uk/healthandlifesciences/cgi-bin/browse.pl?id=33777&gateway=nmap: Intute: Health &Life Sciences

www.museumoflondon.org.uk: Museum of London

www.statistics.gov.uk: National Statistics Online

www.health-promotion.cdd.nhs.uk/index.cfm?articleid=3545: NHS Health Promotion

www.jobs.nhs.uk/: NHS Jobs

www.niscc.info: Northern Ireland Social Care Council

www.nmc-uk.org: Nursing & Midwifery Council

www.rcn.org.uk: Royal College of Nursing

www.rnib.org.uk: Royal National Institute of the Blind

www.rnid.org.uk: Royal National Institute for the Deaf

www.skillsforcare.org.uk: Sector Skills Council for Care

www.skillsforhealth.org.uk: Sector Skills Council for Health

www.scils.co.uk: Social Care Information and Learning Services

www.scie.org.uk: Social Care Institute for Excellence

www.sasi.group.shef.ac.uk: Social and Spatial Inequalities Research Group

www.society.guardian.co.uk: The Guardian

www.who.int: The World Health Organisation

www.parliament.uk: UK Parliament

Index

Note: page numbers in *italics* refer to diagrams, figures and photographs. Page numbers in **bold** refer to text boxes, coloured blocks and tables.